RESTORED

Moving from Just Surviving to Healed and Rejoicing

Sherri Watt

RESTORED

Moving from Just Surviving to Healed and Rejoicing
Copyright © 2020 Sherri Watt

Requests for information should be addressed to:

Sherri Watt
P.O. Box 6967
Lee's Summit, MO 64063

www.sherriwatt.com

Cover Photography, 2020 by Meredith Necole Photography (m-n-photograhy.com)
All rights reserved. Used with permission.

Copyedited by Jennifer Edwards (jedwardsediting.net)

All Scripture quotations, unless otherwise indicated, are taken from the Holy Bible, New International Version®, NIV® Copyright ©1973, 1978, 1984, 2011 by Biblica, Inc.® Used by permission. All rights reserved worldwide.

Scripture quotations marked NLT are taken from the *Holy Bible*, New Living Translation, copyright © 1996, 2004, 2015 by Tyndale House Foundation. Used by permission of Tyndale House Publishers, Inc., Carol Stream, Illinois 60188. All rights reserved.

Scripture quotations marked NKJV are taken from the *Holy Bible, New King James Version®*, NKJV®, Copyright © 1982 by Thomas Nelson, Inc. Used by permission. All rights reserved.

Scripture quotations marked MSG are taken from *THE MESSAGE*, copyright © 1993, 2002, 2018 by Eugene H. Peterson. Used by permission of NavPress. All rights reserved. Represented by Tyndale House Publishers, Inc.

All rights reserved. No part of this publication may be reproduced, stored in a retrieval system, or transmitted in any form or by any means – electronic, mechanical, photocopy, recording, or any other – except for brief quotations in printed reviews, without the prior permission of the publisher.

Printed in the United States of America

Contents

ITS TIME TO UNPACK YOUR BAGGAGE..1

SESSION ONE
Do You Really Need Help?...3

SESSION TWO
Freedom Is Available..17

SESSION THREE
God's Plan Is Restoration...23

SESSION FOUR
Decide to Do A New Thing..33

SESSION FIVE
Learning to Trust God..43

SESSION SIX
Understanding Where We Came From..53

SESSION SEVEN
Dealing with the Dysfunction of Our Family..63

SESSION EIGHT
Healing Painful Memories...71

SESSION NINE
We Were Created to Be Dependent..81

SESSION TEN
Knowing Your Identity and Value..89

It's Time to Unpack Your Baggage

We all have a past. Despite how capable our parents were, none of us escape childhood without some type of baggage because no one parents perfectly. It's inevitable that everyone enters adulthood with at least a little damage. It's just the way it is.

When we don't deal with our past or repair any incorrect thinking we've picked up during childhood, we end up feeling unfulfilled, discontented, and fragmented. It is at this point we begin searching for a way to cope with our dissatisfaction.

Leaving behind the damage—the baggage caused by childhood trauma, abuse, sexual abuse, abandonment, or neglect—doesn't happen by pretending it never existed. Denial doesn't heal trauma. Instead, it creates slaves to addiction, disassociation, eating disorders, grief, depression, over-spending, self-mutilation, risky sexual behavior, and relationship dysfunction.

In an attempt to manage our residual feelings, we look to coping mechanisms which eventually take over our life. Dependence on anything other than God is a slippery slope that speeds out of our control very quickly. Destructive thinking leads to overwhelming strongholds that seem impossible to overcome.

While striving for happiness, we sometimes end up where we never intended to be. I know this because it's my story. Due to stuffing away childhood sexual abuse for years, denial had me dragging my baggage around, ending up in one ruinous circumstance after another. My plans often ended badly. But God's plan never includes us arriving at such destructive destinations. Most of us can bring good out of good, but only God can bring good out of bad. God did that with my life; he took the landscape of a ruined life and created new life out of what seemed dead. This is why I write and share the way to freedom.

Paul writes in 2 Corinthians 1:4, "He comforts us in all our troubles so that we can comfort others. When they are troubled, we will be able to give them the same comfort God has given us." (NLT)

God is always willing to show us the way out of our ruins. He uses those he has already restored to light the way for us. *His plan is always restoration*. He wants to restore us to a joy-filled life through a relationship with Jesus Christ.

Don't get me wrong—having a relationship with Jesus doesn't mean we will never struggle again. It means, with dependence on the Holy Spirit, we can have the joy of the Lord, even in the midst of turmoil. Yes, restoration comes through Jesus Christ alone.

What we know is that God is big. He is powerful. He is supernatural. He can do great healing in us if we have the faith and courage to face our problems. Self-help tools are great for creating understanding, but only Jesus can heal. He can break any bondage. He can change any destructive behavior. He can repair any damaged thinking. He can put new feelings to old memories. Without Jesus, we are stuck in the mud of dysfunction with no hope for change. With him, change is possible. The past doesn't have to predict the future.

In this course, there are ten lessons comprised of impactful content with reflection questions at the end of each session. Reflect on what you have learned, then go deeper by answering the thought-provoking questions. These questions are designed to allow you to process your past individually and find healing through seeking God's input. As you work through the lessons, lean on Jesus. Great freedom takes a greater power than human effort can provide. Jesus provides the supernatural power needed if you abide in him and let him lead.

I am praying for you, my friend. *Stay the course. Stay faithful. Jesus will make things happen.*

Thank you for trusting me by choosing *Restored*. May you see great freedom established in your life.

SESSION ONE

Do You Really Need Help?

Who really wants to rely on outside help to manage their life? No one does. We think we can handle things on our own. Even when life spirals out of control, we hang onto control with every ounce of our strength. Who wants to look like they have problems? And if you do accept help, won't everyone around you know and think poorly of you?

We just don't like to think we need help. As long as we can get away with the denial, we can stay on the surface and pretend through life. We say things to ourselves like, "I got this." "It's not really as bad as people think." "I've got it under control." "I don't need anyone to help me; I can do it on my own." These are just a few of the lies we tell ourselves as our life fragments and spirals out of control.

Our life can spiral out of control like a spinning top from things that seems small and insignificant. Like the pin of a top starts the spinning, so do our small indiscretions. Small things, like taking the twenty out of your billfold, promising yourself that it's all you will spend as you enter the casino. Choosing to just eat one cupcake out of the dozen you are buying. Or stopping to have just one drink at happy hour, promising yourself it won't be an all-nighter.

The lies grow gradually. Just like the spinning top, the progression grows, expands, wobbles, and gets to the point where it is too big and unstable to handle.

Spinning tops usually end in our unraveling. The trip to the casino didn't go as expected and now the rent money is gone. The dozen cupcakes you ate have left you physically and emotionally ill. All you meant to do was instill a little discipline when your anger rose up, obscenities came out, and now the kids are crying.

The thread gets pulled and the hem unravels. Everything is a little more than we expected, and before we know it, all the hem is gone. The thread is gone, and our favorite shirt has a ragged edge.

Sometimes our response to the unraveling thread shows us how much help we really need. It's the response of denial that reveals when it's time to go get help.

See if you recognize yourself in the following scenarios. Do you see yourself in the way the problems are responded to?

I just lost my job…

> But it wasn't my fault I couldn't make it to work every day.
> I couldn't help being late all the time.
> Maybe if I lived closer… if they weren't so strict.
> Why does it matter if I'm late? I get the job done and work hard when I'm there.

My relationships are toxic but…

> I don't mean to scream obscenities at my kids, but I just can't control my emotions right now.
> I can't help it when my anger erupts; if people wouldn't make me so mad, I would be fine.

I'm in bankruptcy…

> But it's not my fault; I deserved a bigger house and a boat.
> I know I shouldn't have spent all my money, shopped online, but the pressure is too much at work and I needed relief.

My family won't talk to me anymore…

> But it's not my fault; they deserve my anger.
> I was in jail again, and I called them, but they wouldn't pick up the phone. They deserved my response when I got out.

My drinking/eating habits are killing me…

> It's not that bad; I just drink to take the edge off after a hard day.
> I'm okay. The doctor doesn't know what he is talking about. I know he says my health is in jeopardy, but I feel fine most of the time.

My marriage is lifeless and over…

> It is what it is. We don't get along, so it's easier to just ignore one another.
> I'm just not that happy in my marriage. I deserve better.

I feel alone and lost…

> No one wants to be my friend. No one likes me.

Do you see the pattern emerging? The pattern in the responses?

"It's not my fault."
"I'm not responsible."
"It's not that bad."
"They made me do it."
"If only they would…"

See, here's the problem. If the circumstance you find yourself in isn't your fault, then the responsibility to fix it isn't yours either. Any consequences for bad behavior or lack of happiness belong to someone else. *They* should fix the problem. But they won't. *They can't!* They have their own lives to deal with.

When you make statements like the ones previous, what you are really saying is this:

"I accept no responsibility for my actions or the outcome in my life. Life can just keep happening to me and I will accept it. Maybe things will get better on their own."

But they won't.

When things begin to unravel, it's time to face the facts.

Denial Doesn't Work

Like I said before, denial reveals when it's time to go get help. Denying a problem exists or blaming others does nothing but prolong and increase the problem. If you stay in denial, you can deny any responsibility to improve your outcome and future. And if it's someone else's fault then there's no need for you to change.

A denial is when you say things like, "I've got my life under control." "I can handle this on my own." "I don't have a problem. They have a problem, not me." Denial doesn't work. Not if you want things in your life to be different. Not if you want the pain of the past to stop nagging at you and impacting your today.

Do you feel your toes being squished right now? Have I stepped too hard? If I have, it likely means you need to come out of denial and get to work finding better in your life. You may be able to live in this denial and be able to function mediocre for a short period of time, but eventually, reality makes it impossible to stay there. If you refuse to deal with reality, problems get bigger and bigger. In life, we can only change the behavior of ourselves. And it starts with getting out of denial.

The first step out of denial is learning to take responsibility for your actions and problems. This is one of the great universal principles about how the world works. In the Bible, God reiterates it through Paul in Galatians:

> *"Do not be deceived: God cannot be mocked. A man reaps what he sows. Whoever sows to please their flesh, from the flesh will reap destruction; whoever sows to please the Spirit, from the Spirit will reap eternal life. Let us not become weary of doing good, for at the proper time we will reap a harvest if we do not give up."*
> (Galatians 6:7–9)

We reap what we sow. Every action you take in life has a reaction. It has a consequence. You cannot act on something without there being a consequence in return. Most often, good actions create good consequences, and bad actions create bad consequences. Usually, your actions will carry the appropriate consequences that belong with them. And consequences never impact just you, they hurt everyone around you. Even when you think you are managing it, there will be consequences paid by the people around you.

If your parents didn't teach you to evaluate the consequences of your actions before executing them, then teaching yourself to do so in adulthood is your responsibility. You now have to teach yourself to own your own actions, feelings, and problems, and to deal with the consequences that come with them.

If you want permanent change in your life, begin by saying to yourself, "I have a problem and I need help. I need to deal with my problem. No matter why or how it started, I am now an adult and getting over the past is my responsibility." You can do it; you've got this.

Deal with the Baggage from Your Past

Our pasts have a lot of baggage in them that can be very heavy and weigh you down. Sometimes your past weighs so much that you can't move any further. That's why you have to put it down so you can heal the baggage from your past. If you have dysfunction in your family (which we all do), then you have baggage from your past that needs healing. Sometimes we stuff and ignore our past and it creeps out in destructive behaviors. Where your problems started may not be your fault, but how you deal with them in adulthood is still your responsibility.

If you stuff your problems or deny the past, it will eventually come out in relationship damage. Likely, some type of your own dysfunction will be passed on to the next generation through you unless you do the work of healing yourself. Your children pick up dysfunction without ever being taught. Even with the best parenting, if you carry your dysfunctional past, they too will carry some of your baggage as they grow up.

To move forward, you will need to address the past. It's your responsibility to make your life better. You cannot expect someone else to fix things for you. Your problems and how you now live with them rest on your shoulders. Face the past now to have a healthy, productive, joy-filled future, instead of continually struggling through tortured feelings.

Decide you are in control of your own ability to move into healing and choose to be responsible for the way you behave. Decide you are in control of your own ability to move into healing and choose to be responsible for the way you behave. This means you have to:

> Own your talk, words, actions, feelings, attitudes, and thoughts.
>
> Own what you say and how you say it to other people.
>
> Own when you give yourself permission to get angry.
>
> Own when you let yourself get mad and act out by yelling at someone.
>
> Own feeling jealous or feeling justified to do what you know you shouldn't.
>
> Own when your attitude stinks and you're ugly because of it.
>
> Own the lustful thoughts that run through your head that you camp on. (Yes, you are even responsible for your thoughts and how you react to them.)

The "blame game" gets you nowhere but stuck in your problem.

> *You blame, you stay stuck.*
>
>> So if you want to get unstuck…
>>
>>> …if you want to stop cycling in the pain of the past;
>>>
>>> …if you want to stop feeling the way you're feeling;
>>>
>>> …if you want to stop being damaged and broken…
>>>
>>>> …then there can be no more denial.
>
> No more blaming the people in your past that hurt you.
>
> No more allowing yourself to be a victim.
> No more ignoring the problem.

It's time to look yourself in the mirror and say, "I have a problem and I'm going to get help."

Where Help Comes From

"I lift up my eyes to the mountains—where does my help come from? My help comes from the Lord, the Maker of heaven and earth." (Psalm 121:1–2)

Our help comes from the Lord, from God. How do you know if you need God to help you? It's when nothing else seems to work. You handle things without God by giving no consideration to what the Bible says, refusing to address problems in prayer. At first, you think you have the power to handle things by yourself. "I'll just think better, feel better, or act better."

You may not rationally think or say "I don't need God," but by trying to do life on your own, you're saying to God, "I don't need you." When we do this, what we are really saying is we are big enough to be our own god. We are telling the Creator of the universe that we have more knowledge, more understanding, and more ability when it comes to fixing us. That we know what we need better than God does. We understand ourselves better. We know better what our abilities are. We can be our own god.

But does this really work? Does the pot know better than the potter? Can the painting really advise the painter? Does the house tell the builder, "I can fix myself," when the roof leaks or the pipes break? Do we really know better than the one who put us together? Can you or I speak something into existence like God can? Can we tell the wind to blow on one side and then quiet the waters on the other? Can we really be our own god?

While being your own god may gain you a small degree of success, this level of success is insufficient for true freedom. You may even overcome some of the issues you have in your life. But ultimately, if you want to gain complete freedom from your past, you need a God bigger than yourself.

To overcome great hurt in your life takes great power. It takes supernatural power. Who has more power than the Creator of everything? Who other than God has the power to cause a man's heart to change completely in just the blink of an eye? Who else can do the supernatural? Who else can do the miraculous?

No one... only God can do the miraculous. If healing is what you seek, it's going to take the supernatural help of God, of Jesus himself. This is who our help will comes from.

Jesus Has Great Power

We, indeed, need a trustworthy, wise, great and powerful God to overcome our hurt. But is Jesus that kind of God? Is he trustworthy and wise? What makes him so great? Does he have that kind of power? Consider these verses and see what the scriptures say. They beautifully answer these questions.

> "For to us a child is born, to us a son is given, and the government will be on his shoulders. And he will be called Wonderful Counselor, Mighty God, Everlasting Father, Prince of Peace." (Isaiah 9:6)

> "Who has known the mind of the Lord? Or who has been his Counselor?" (Romans 11:34)

> "Great is our Lord and mighty in power; his understanding has no limit." (Psalm 147:5)

> "Then Jesus came to them and said, 'All authority in heaven and on earth has been given to me.'" (Matthew 28:18)

> "I pray that the eyes of your heart may be enlightened in order that you may know the hope to which he has called you, the riches of his glorious inheritance in his holy people, and his incomparably great power for us who believe. That power is the same as the mighty strength he exerted when he raised Christ from the dead and seated him at his right hand in the heavenly realms, far above all rule and authority, power and dominion, and every name that is invoked, not only in the present age but also the one to come." (Ephesians 1:18–21)

These Scriptures show the following about Jesus's power:

- The government will be upon his shoulders.
- His name is Wonderful.
- He is the first and greatest Counselor.
- He is the Mighty God.
- He is everlasting (never-ending, no beginning and no ending).
- He is the Prince of Peace.
- Who knows his mind or can be his counselor? No one.
- He is mighty in power.
- His understanding is infinite (unending understanding, all-knowing).
- All authority in heaven and on earth was given to him.
- Jesus exerted power to raise himself from the dead and is now seated at the Father's right hand in the heavenly realm, far above all rule, authority, power, or dominion.

According to these verses, there is none with power higher or vaster than Jesus. Since all Scripture is God-breathed, it is truth and can be trusted (2 Timothy 3:16). We can rest in what it tells us about the power of Jesus Christ. We can be assured of his ability to heal our wounds. God is plenty big enough to handle our problems. He has ultimate power and every understanding about what we need.

Does Jesus Care Enough about Me to Help?

I know it doesn't seem like a God of such great power and fame would help us. After all, we are so microscopic in the scope of his vastness. Just the vastness of his creating power when you look at the universe is mind boggling. Compared to his magnitude, each of us individually is so infinitesimally insignificant. We are nothing but a wisp of air in the frame of his immenseness.

We can sometimes get it in our head that he is too far away or too high up to care enough to intervene for us on a personal level. Why would he care about one small person of such lowly significance? "He probably doesn't know I exist," we say. "Would he care enough to help me?" "As insignificant as I am, as many mistakes as I have made, as unimportant as I am, would Jesus really care that much about me to heal me?"

You may be thinking Jesus could never forgive a person like you. Maybe you're thinking about all the mistakes you've made, and the gravity of it weighs you down. How could a holy, vast, big, important God care about someone messed up, broken, and flawed?

That's what I thought until he showed me how he really felt about the wounded and broken. His whole mission was focused on helping people:

"He heals the brokenhearted and binds up their wounds." (Psalm 147:3)

"When the teachers of the law who were Pharisees saw him eating with the sinners and tax collectors, they asked his disciples: 'Why does he eat with tax collectors and sinners?' On hearing this, Jesus said to them, 'It is not the healthy who need a doctor, but the sick. I have not come to call the righteous, but sinners.'" (Mark 2:16–17)

Jesus came to help those who needed help, not those who had it all together. He came for people with problems—like you and like me.

But what about the worthless?

What about the abused?

What about those left feeling neglected?

What about those who have felt abandoned?

What about the women who have given themselves away to men over and over?

What about the woman who trades in sex for a living?

What about the woman making a living dancing on a pole?

What about those who left their children for drugs?

What about the woman who aborted her baby?

What about the woman who aborted multiple babies?

What about those still stuck in their memories of abuse?

What about those who wake up in a cold sweat from nightmares of the past?

What about the one suffering from PTSD cause by trauma?

What about the woman living a homosexual lifestyle?

What about those battling addiction?

What about people who feel they have nothing worth redeeming in them?

What about people who feel like they have done everything wrong in their life?

What about those who have made every mistake and have cared for no one but themselves?

What about anyone who ever felt like they did anything wrong?

What if they really did everything wrong?

What about the people who really believed and asked Jesus to take away the pain and hurt from the past?

What about when they were disappointed because they saw no miracle take place?

Did he really come to help women like these? Yes, he did. Luke 7:36–47 tells a beautiful story about a woman so beaten down by life that she'd forgotten her worth. The circumstances of the world she lived in were ugly at best and brutal in their worst. She was lost, broken, and hurt. But Jesus didn't see her that way.

> When one of the Pharisees invited Jesus to have dinner with him, he went to the Pharisee's house and reclined at the table. A woman in that town who lived a sinful life learned that Jesus was eating at the Pharisee's house, so she came there with an alabaster jar of perfume. As she stood behind him at his feet weeping, she began to wet his feet with her tears. Then she wiped them with her hair, kissed them and poured perfume on them.
>
> When the Pharisee who had invited him saw this, he said to himself, "If this man were a prophet, he would know who is touching him and what kind of woman she is – she is a sinner."
> Jesus answered him, "Simon, I have something to tell you." "Tell me teacher," he said.
>
> "Two people owed money to a certain moneylender. One owed him five hundred denarii, and the other fifty. Neither of them had the money to pay him back, so he forgave the debts of both. Now which of them will love him more?"
>
> Simon replied, "I suppose the one who had the bigger debt forgiven."
>
> "You have judged correctly," Jesus said. Then he turned toward the woman and said to Simon, "Do you see this woman? I came into your house. You did not give me any water for my feet, but she wet my feet with her tears and wiped them with hair. You did not give me a kiss, but this woman, from the time I entered, has not stopped kissing my feet. You did not put oil on my head, but she has poured perfume on my feet. Therefore, I tell you her many sins have been forgiven – as her great love has shown. But whoever has been forgiven little loves little." (Luke 7:36–47)

Jesus answered all our questions in his response to the sinful woman with the alabaster jar. You see, that sinful woman was just like you and me. She didn't know her worth to Jesus. She had been used and abused over and over. Her own internal dialog belittling herself ran on constant repeat. She felt despicable and unworthy. She valued herself with so little esteem that she had prostituted herself to man after man. Everyone knew her and considered her value to be that of a filthy rag. She was something to be used and disposed of. Not valued as a person but as an object.

Dear one, have people looked down on you or judged you like the righteous, pious Pharisee's did the sinful woman? Have you believed you have no worth? Have you believed you could never be truly loved? You've made too many mistakes, or the problems seem too big to fix? Have you believed you are too broken and unfixable? That nothing will work, or you won't make it through it? Have you believed and been disappointed when God didn't fix it the way expected?

Jesus didn't see the woman with the alabaster jar as beyond help or love. He doesn't see you that way either. He wants to wipe away the tears and say, "Stand up and live in who I say you are, not what others think of you." He wants to fix what's broken and hold you all the way through it. But like the woman, you have to place it all at his feet and let him take you through the rough stuff. It's humbling. It's raw. It's complete honesty. Definitely not a quick fix or magic formula.

He cared about every tear she suffered through and weeps with your tears too. He doesn't just care about the broken and struggling, he chases after them. His heart grieves as he watches you heave through the weight of carrying your load of pain every day. He wants to take it from you and rid you of it permanently. But you will have to face the feelings of the past to overcome them.

He cares. He cares to the point of sweating blood in the garden of Gethsemane as he prayed for strength to follow through and lay his life down for you. Jesus loves you. He loves you broken. He loves you filthy. He loves you hurting. He loves you strong-willed. He loves you crying alone. He just plain *loves* you.

He came. He died. Not so you could just survive this lifetime on earth, but so you could *really* live. So you could live *free*. So you could put all your excuses down and do the work of healing.

Yes, dear one, he really does care about you. His power is great enough to remove your baggage and heal your past. You can trust him to carry your load while he grates a new path to joy instead of the pain and sadness. Trust him and let him guide you there.

SESSION ONE REFLECTION QUESTIONS

How do you respond when things don't go your way?

Do you see yourself blaming others instead of taking responsibility in some areas of your life? Explain how?

What consequences have others dealt with for your bad behavior?

In what ways do you need to begin taking responsibility?

Describe a time when you tried to handle things on your own and it had bad consequences?

How are you trying to be your own god?

Where in your life do you need supernatural power?

Explain Psalm 147:3 in your own words. How can you apply it to your life?

Explain Mark 2:16–17 in your own words. How you can apply it to your life?

How do you relate to the story of the sinful woman with the alabaster jar?

SESSION TWO

Freedom Is Available

So often we look for answers from programs and self-help tools. There are many great ones out there. Unfortunately, the majority of them advertise their program or tool as having the answer to help people heal, essentially using God (or Jesus) as a tool. Reality is actually backwards; Jesus helps people heal, while programs and books are merely tools he uses. This lesson will take you through the idea of breaking free, to achieve complete and total freedom in life. It is Jesus who brings complete freedom.

"To the Jews who had believed him, Jesus said, 'If you hold to my teachings, you are really my disciples. Then you will know the truth, and the truth will set you free.'" (John 8:31–32)

To activate freedom, three conditions need to be met:

1. *"To the Jews who had believed him."* Notice to whom Jesus is speaking—the people who believed him. So the first condition is faith, the belief that Jesus has the ability to change things. To be set free, we must first believe him—to believe he is who he says he is. Faith is paramount.

2. *"If you hold true to my teachings, you are really my disciples."* The second condition to our freedom is knowing what Jesus teaches and then holding true to it. This demonstrates you are really a disciple. What does it mean to be a real disciple? It's knowing what Jesus teaches and living by it.

Jesus spoke these words as the twelve disciples traveled with him day and night. They followed him everywhere. As they preached the good news throughout the land, they made new disciples who believed in Jesus. Once a disciple, they were required to follow and learn his teachings, then hold true to them.

3. *"Then you will know the truth, and the truth will set you free."* The third condition is to know the truth. The truth is in the word of God. It is getting to know the mind and heart of God through understanding what's written in his Word, the Bible. God's Word is living, meaning it is relevant to us today. And it is powerful, so powerful, it transforms us. As we read the truth in the Bible, God uses it to transform our mind and heal our soul. The "Truth" in this

Scripture is Jesus Christ. Therefore, if Jesus Christ makes you free, you shall be free indeed.

Great Freedom Takes Great Power

The trauma many of us experience in childhood is too big for mere man to heal. Great pain and hurt takes a greater power than we are able to muster up by ourselves. Power to heal our thinking and change our feelings takes *supernatural* power. It takes an all-powerful, supernatural force to remove the hurts that evil created and to bring complete freedom from them. Is this the type of healing you are in need of? Be encouraged because real help is available. Jesus is the living God and has the transforming power to change and heal people. And he wants to use his power to help you.

In John 8:31–32, Jesus was trying desperately to spread his freedom message to the people. He was saying, "Look to me; I have the power to set you free." The next two verses show that the disciples simply didn't get it.

"They answered him, 'We are Abraham's descendants and have never been slaves to anyone. How can you say that we shall be set free?' Jesus replied, 'Very truly I tell you, everyone who sins is a slave to sin.'" (John 8:33–34)

The Jews didn't understand what he meant by truth setting them free. They questioned him, "Why would we need to be set free when we've never been slaves?" They were looking at spiritual truth with earthly eyes. In Old Testament history, God had made their ancestor Abraham a promise: his people would be God's people. They were given a great inheritance. The Jews had never considered themselves as slaves. They were children of God. Their understanding of freedom didn't reach past their daily life.

Prophecy had predicted a Messiah (King) would come from their blood line and reign. What they didn't understand was this was a spiritual prediction not an earthly one. They were waiting for their king to come and reign in Jerusalem, to take over power from the Romans. They wouldn't have considered themselves slaves but children of a godly king.

Jesus's reply was very simple… everyone sins, and therefore, everyone is a slave to their sin. He had come to free people from being a slave to sin. He had come to bring spiritual freedom to every sinner who accepted his help.

Everyone's Journey Is Different

Each of us has a different path to healing. There are no two journeys that match. Jesus knows what you need to be restored. The power to transform comes from

Christ. He makes it personal. Healing is personal and individual because every person's needs are unique. Although we might have some of the same experiences, our needs are never identical.

We want a quick-fix. We want a simple math kind of answer to an exponential equation. I wish it were that easy. Develop the perfect formula for the problems each of us face and apply it. Voila', fixed. It's easy to think, "Give me the steps so I can get this done, and the faster the better." We all want the struggle to be over. Some of the information we need is common, but most of what each of us need is individual. Therefore, no two stories are the same. How we feel and our ways of coping will be different. Because no two individuals are identical, there will never be just one best way for everyone to heal. Only Jesus knows what you need and can give it to you exactly when you need it. Jesus Christ is the "Son" John talked about in the Scripture, and he will set you free.

"Now a slave has no permanent place in the family, but a son belongs to it forever. So if the Son sets you free, you will be free indeed." (John 8:35–36)

Here's the amazing thing about God; he makes promises and then he keeps them. He made an incredible promise right here in this Scripture. Jesus explained that a slave doesn't have a permanent place in the family, but a son does. A son is different; he belongs to the family forever. Nothing can take away the heritage of a son. Since Jesus is the Son of God, he can make this permanent promise concerning our freedom. If he grants it, God will make it come to pass.

Here's the promise: If you believe in him and hold to his teachings, he will give you freedom from your sin, and when he sets you free, you are truly and completely free. He has a journey to freedom set before each one of us. We need only to join him to begin unlocking the chains.

Healing Takes Time

Have you ever wondered, "Will I ever be better?" I did. I wanted complete restoration immediately. I got saved and thought, "All my past problems should be gone." After all, 2 Corinthians 5:17 (NKJV) says,

"Therefore, if anyone is in Christ, he is a new creation; old things have passed away; behold all things have become new."

As a new believer, we have become a new creation, but it's just the beginning of rebirth. Although God now sees our status as clean and new, we still live in the mind and body of our old self. Our thinking is still flawed because our sin nature is still intact. Depending on when you make the decision to follow Christ quantifies the degree of work you'll do to overhaul your old life and thinking patterns.

Romans 12:2 says it all.

"Do not conform to the pattern of this world, but be transformed by the renewing of your mind. Then you will be able to test and approve what God's will is—his good, pleasing and perfect will."

In other words, do not be like this world, but be transformed. If you trace the word "transformed" back to the Greek origin, it means "metamorphosis." Metamorphosis was something we learned in science class. The caterpillar's form is completely changed into a butterfly during this process. He goes into a chrysalis (cocoon) as a sixteen-legged caterpillar, looking much like a worm, and emerges five to twenty-one days later as a multicolored, winged butterfly ready to take flight. It's amazing!

Our form is completely changed too. How? By the renewing of our mind. It takes time and effort to change the messages that have been implanted in your computer-like brain throughout your whole life. It takes time, some good tools, and a powerful God who is willing to use his power to transform you supernaturally.

We all want to slap on a Band-Aid and get on with life. But God's not an advocate of Band-Aid freedom. He provides long-term freedom. His freedom goes the distance and sticks for the long haul.

It's taken each of us a long time to do damage to our life and thinking. Occasionally God does the miraculous and we get instant healing. There is nothing wrong with asking for a miracle. Most often, though, he answers us by letting us walk through the fog while guiding our way.

Don't be discouraged. God knows when you need to walk through the restoration process in order to unlearn incorrect thinking patterns and behaviors. He wants your character to be changed permanently so you stop struggling with old desires. And that takes time. Your journey to healing is the way you make those permanent changes.

My friend, Jesus is waiting for the opportunity to prove his transforming power can work for you. He stands at the door knocking (Revelation 3:20), waiting for you to answer so he can start the process of setting you free. I know it's scary, and it feels risky to trust what feels unknown, but give him a chance. I know it's true because he set me free. And he will set you free too.

SESSION TWO REFLECTION QUESTIONS

Dispelling the internal message that your past must be kept a secret is paramount to freedom. This week, choose someone safe you could share your story with. Write their name here.

If you don't feel strong enough yet to share your story out loud, write it down here or on a separate piece of paper.

Why have you chosen now to change things in your life?

How can you apply the message of John 8:31–36 to your own life?

Describe what freedom looks like for you?

Second Corinthians 5:17 shares that you are a new creation. With this understanding, how might it change your thinking?

Romans 12:2 talks about transformation coming through renewing your mind. In what way do you need God to begin to change your thinking?

SESSION THREE

God's Plan Is Restoration

I n the beginning...

The first chapter of Genesis gives the beginning account of creation and the origin of both man and woman. God created them, male and female, and gave them each a job and responsibility.

"Then God said, 'Let us make mankind in our image, in our likeness, so that they may rule over the fish in the sea and the birds in the sky, over the livestock and all the wild animals, and over all the creatures that move along the ground.' So God created mankind in His own image, in the image of God He created them; male and female He created them. God blessed them and said to them, 'Be fruitful and increase in number; fill the earth and subdue it. Rule over the fish of the sea and the birds in the sky and over every living creature that moves on the ground.'" (Genesis 1:26–28)

When you get to the second chapter of Genesis, the story gets more personal and the focus turns directly toward God's design and instruction for man and woman. Pay particular attention to the description in verse seven.

"Then the Lord God formed a man from the dust of the ground and breathed into his nostrils the breath of life, and man became a living being." (Genesis 2:7)

God breathed into the nostrils of Adam. He breathed himself, his own breath into man, and the man came alive. Adam is in this great garden, the Garden of Eden. Then God puts him to work. He gives him fulfillment through responsibility for tending the garden and a purpose, naming all the animals. Whoa. Wait a minute. Every other creature has a mate and is procreating. As Adam spends day after day appropriately naming each creature, there is both a male and female. Where is his mate? He must have begun to wonder. Did he bring up the topic to God as they walked through the garden together? With such a vast number of living creatures there are on the earth, Adam must have spent years naming those animals. It makes me curious how long he named animals before it dawned on him that he had no mate for himself!

"But for Adam no suitable helper was found. So the Lord God caused the man to fall into a deep sleep; and while he was sleeping, he took one of the man's ribs and then closed up the place with flesh. Then the Lord God made a woman from the rib he had taken out of the man, and he brought her to the man. The man said, 'This is now bone of

my bones and flesh of my flesh; she shall be called woman, for she was taken out of man.'" (Genesis 2:20–23)

For our purposes of restoration, there are three very important points we need to focus on. They have huge implications for you and me.

1. *Mankind was created in the image of God.* No other creature, including angelic beings, have ever been created in God's image. We were molded to be different than any other creation manufactured by the living God. We were created to reflect God by our character.

2. *Mankind was brought to life with the very breath of God breathed into his nostrils.* God put himself, his own essence, into us to place his own image within us. This means we have a piece of God within us. Not that we *are* God or gods ourselves, but part of God lives within us. The part of God which was breathed into and is living in mankind is called our spirit. Before sin entered the world, our spirit connected us directly to God himself.

3. When we talk of mankind—the image of God in mankind, and the breath of life in mankind—it *includes both male and female.* Even though the breath of God wasn't blown directly into woman, she was taken from man who already had God's breath within him.

One Rule Is Given in the Garden

Genesis 2:16–17. God puts the man in a beautiful garden. Gives him the care and upkeep of the garden. Tells him "Enjoy the garden. But there's just one thing. See this tree over here? It's the tree of knowledge of good and evil. Do not eat from it. There is only one rule, but it comes with dire consequences. If you fail to follow this one rule, you will surely die." Then God goes on to make Adam a helpmate.

Man and woman. They are set for life. Great food to eat, because all the fruit trees are succulent and delicious. Beautiful tropical weather. Calm breezes. Surrounded by beauty everywhere they looked. No loneliness because they have each other for company. Connected to God on a personal level. Companionship as they walk with God in the garden together. Complete and whole, feeling no shame.

"Adam and his wife were both naked, and they felt no shame." (Genesis 2:25)

The Fall of Mankind

They felt no shame. They were complete, but they didn't stay that way.

> *"Now the serpent was more crafty than any of the wild animals the Lord God had made. He said to the woman, 'Did God really say, "You must not eat from any tree in the garden"?' The woman said to the serpent, 'We may eat fruit from the trees in the garden, but God did say, "You must not eat fruit from the tree that is in the middle of the garden, and you must not touch it, or you will die."'*
>
> *'You will not surely die,' the serpent said to the woman. 'For God knows that when you eat of it your eyes will be opened, and you will be like God, knowing good and evil.'*
>
> *When the woman saw that the fruit of the tree was good for food and pleasing to the eye, and also desirable for gaining wisdom, she took some and ate it. She also gave some to her husband, who was with her, and he ate it. Then the eyes of both of them were opened, and they realized they were naked; so they sewed fig leaves together and made coverings for themselves."* (Genesis 3:1–7)

Satan was crafty. He twisted the truth. He flipped God's words around just a fraction and played the game of *manipulation*, the game he's most famous for. His rewording of God's instructions made Eve question. "Did God really say that? Would God hold out on us? If the fruit of that tree is good for gaining wisdom, why wouldn't God want us to have knowledge and wisdom?"

All these questions ultimately lead to the big question. Is God really good? Does he really have *my* best interest at heart with this rule? After all, the fruit looks good enough; it looks just as juicy and attractive as the rest of the fruit in the garden, what's the difference? Plus it will make me wiser. Doesn't God want me to be wise?

Eve took a piece of fruit and ate it. She gave it to her husband and he ate it too. Their eyes were opened and suddenly they knew they were naked; for the first time, they felt ashamed. Their childlike innocence was gone; they felt the need to cover themselves. The wholeness and perfection created in mankind was broken.

Who knew that a small bite of a piece of fruit could do so much damage? God did. How relevant this applies to our lives today. What sometimes looks like a small compromise ends up leading to big trouble. It looks like such a small choice, but is it really? Sometimes a small compromise in your values can take you spiraling down a path you don't want to go. If you compromise in small ways, eventually you may find yourself compromising in bigger ways.

Eve compromised on God's one rule, then turned to her husband and he joined in. When we mess up, we rarely do it alone. We recruit others to travel the road with us. Our mistakes are like a shotgun shell. Once the buckshot leaves the barrel of a shotgun, it separates and sprays out, hitting a wide area around the target and does a lot of damage. Our mistakes can spray like buckshot from a shotgun. There may only be one shell in the chamber but the damage is severe.

Adam and Eve Felt Ashamed

After eating the fruit which God had forbidden them to enjoy, the one feeling we are told about is their shame. In fact, their shame was so great, they took fig leaves and made themselves coverings out of fig leaves. Can't you just picture them? First looking at each other and this whole new feeling that is taking over their emotions. Then looking down at their own naked body and trying to strategically place their hands and arms over their more private areas. They were trying to cover what now seemed unacceptable to be on display. I get this mental picture that they felt like us when we are naked in the bathroom and our houseguest walks in unexpectedly. Where's the towel?!?! Or the nightmare where you go out in public and realize you are completely naked. You wake up feeling ashamed, awkward, embarrassed, and humiliated. It brings with it a feeling of being totally exposed.

God Responds to Their Shame

"Then the man and his wife heard the sound of the LORD GOD as he was walking in the garden in the cool of the day, and they hid from the Lord God among the trees of the garden. But the LORD GOD called to the man, 'Where are you?'

He answered 'I heard you in the garden, and I was afraid because I was naked; so I hid.' And he said 'Who told you that you were naked? Have you eaten from the tree that I commanded you not to eat from?'

The man said, 'The woman you put here with me – she gave me some fruit from the tree, and I ate it.'
Then the LORD GOD said to the woman, 'What is this you have done?'

The woman said, 'The serpent deceived me, and I ate.'" (Genesis 3:8–13)

As they heard God walking in the garden, fear rose up in them and their immediate response was, "Oh, no! Hide!" God called to Adam, "Where are you?"

Funny. Like God didn't know what was going on. God knew. He was giving Adam a chance to come clean. We do it with our children. As parents we want our kids to tell the truth so when they have done something wrong, we give them every opportunity to come clean.

Adam didn't come clean; instead he made excuses, *"I heard you in the garden, and I was afraid because I was naked; so I hid."* God continued to let out the rope Adam kept trying to hang himself with. Throw out more rope, maybe he will come clean now. *"Who told you that you were naked? Have you eaten the fruit you were forbidden to eat?"*

Did Adam finally take responsibility? No, he shifted the blame to Eve, who then blamed the serpent. Adam not only shifted the blame to Eve but reminded God that he was the one who gave her to him in the first place. Pretty bold of Adam, to not only blame his wife but also blame God for his failure. Don't we do the same though? Don't we blame God when life isn't how we expected? When struggles come our way, aren't we asking God why he is punishing us? Sometimes we even blame God when we are the one who created the mess in the first place.

Perhaps if Adam and Eve had owned up to their mistake and readily admitted to their failure, things might have turned out differently. Maybe God would have redeemed them immediately. Instead, their denial of responsibility left them living with the unfortunate consequences of their poor choice.

God's Plan of Restoration

But God isn't willing to let mankind remain in shame forever. He has a plan to restore each one of us into a right relationship with him, where we can walk freely with him while here on this earth. In the chart below, created by Christian counselor, Kandy Jackson, it shows us that before the fall, man was connected to God and felt unashamed. After the fall, man was disconnected and felt shame.
Now God wants to restore us back to the way we were before the fall of mankind.[1] Let's take a look.

MANKIND BEFORE THE FALL	MANKIND AFTER THE FALL	GOD'S PLAN FOR RESTORATION
Connected to God	Disconnected	Re-connected through Jesus
In fellowship w/God	A void within us	Void is filled
Naked but unashamed	Shame-filled	Unashamed
Fulfilled	Always needing more	Fulfilled
Dependent on God	Independent (Self)	Dependent on God
God-centered	Self-centered	God-centered
Trusting God	Trusting other things	Trusting God
Free from sin	Sin-nature within	Sins forgiven in Christ
Not afraid	Fearful	Freed from fear

Before the fall:

Adam and Eve had a natural connection to God. They lived in fellowship, spending daily time with God in the garden. They were naked, but they had a childlike innocence that made them lack any shame. They felt completely fulfilled because their dependence was on God. Their life was centered on

God and they trusted him. They had no sin to deal with or shame to overcome because of it. Because they had no sin or shame, they felt no fear. Fear is a direct consequence of sin. God knew we would struggle with the consequence of fear overwhelmingly, so he repeatedly reminds us in Scripture not to fear. In fact, there are 365 scriptures in the Bible with fear as their context. One reminder for every day of the year.

After the fall:

The first couple experienced the complete opposite of their circumstances they had before the fall. They were disconnected and felt a void within themselves. Shame filled their experience of life. Their level of contentment and fulfillment turned into discontent. The constant need for more then drove them to look for a substitute for God. They became independent, self-centered, and put faith in themselves more than God. Within them was now a nature causing them to desire sin over holiness. Fighting fear became a daily battle.

Restoration:

God has a plan for restoration. His plan is to restore us back to connection and fellowship with himself. We may not end up walking naked in a garden like Adam and Eve were, but we can reclaim the fulfillment, peace, serenity, and purity they once possessed. We can, once again, walk daily with God by trusting him, centering our lives on him. The void in us can be filled by our connection to God and our shame can be removed. Everything lost in the fall can be regained through relationship with Jesus Christ. We only have to believe, receive, and follow his plan to find freedom through his restoration.

Satan Wants Us to Hate God

Satan knows that God's plan for us has always been restoration. He has been trying to cause mankind to hate God from the beginning of time. He wants us to disbelieve God's goodness. He works through our family of origin from the minute we are born trying to discredit God. His attack is planned before our birth. His agenda is to twist our view and misrepresent God so we never consider the love of Jesus Christ in our life. If destroying our family will make us look away from God instead of towards him, Satan will do everything to try and make that happen.

Many people have been hurt greatly by those who were supposed to love them the most. This alone can turn you from God and make you doubt if God is trustworthy. For people who blame God, Satan's plot works. God's plan is not the destruction of anything. It is to bring good to those who love Him.

God knew man would fall from grace. He had a plan. That plan was laid out way before he even began creating. The plan was to provide a way out of sin and into freedom through Jesus Christ.

God knew what mankind would do. He knew with only one rule we would still choose to disobey. He could have scrapped the whole plan, but he didn't. He didn't because we are worth all the trouble he had to go through to redeem us. You are worth it! I am worth it! We are worth enough to him that he fixed the problem himself.

"For God so loved the world that he gave his one and only son, that whoever believes in him shall not perish but have eternal life." (John 3:16)

Our freedom... our restoration, came at great cost to God. It came to us out of great sacrifice. His sacrifice was the Son of God, Jesus Christ dying on a cross so we could be restored.

There is nothing we could sacrifice that would give us the eternal benefit that God offers. Can you imagine sacrificing your own child to give others life? I can't. Maybe you might make that sacrifice for someone who loves you, but would you do it for someone who hates you? Jesus did. He sacrificed his own life even for those who hated him. He did it so all could find freedom.

Freedom for us comes through the ongoing relationship with Jesus Christ. Without the power of Christ, we will always struggle with becoming dependent on the wrong things. Jesus is the answer to find and maintain true healing.

SESSION THREE REFLECTION QUESTIONS

What were man and woman told to do in Genesis 1:28?

What are the three points from Genesis 1:26–2:23 we should focus on? Why do they have significance?

1.

2.

3.

Do you have areas in your life where you are making small compromises in? What are those compromises? How are they affecting people in your life?

In what ways have you lost your childlike innocence?

How has the fall of man affected you personally? What resonated with you most on the list of repercussions for the fall of man?

What part on the restoration list do you need most? Why?

Explain God's plan for restoring each of us. What will you allow him to do in your life?

SESSION FOUR

Decide to Do A New Thing

"Forget the former things; do not dwell on the past. See, I am doing a new thing! Now it springs up; do you not perceive it? I am making a way in the wilderness and streams in the wasteland." (Isaiah 43:18–19)

Have you ever felt hopeless? Does your internal dialog take you down the road of, "What's the use? It's just going to end up the same way as before. I'll try and fail anyway, so why even try?"

Facing the past is scary. Admitting that our problems are adversely impacting us is even scarier. Taking steps to stop unproductive behavior advances us toward change. But in order for true change to happen, we have to want it bad enough to make a commitment. We have to reach the end of contentment, look beyond our own strength, and ready ourselves for change. It may hurt staying where we are, but does it hurt enough to cause action? The pain threshold is different for each individual.

Sometimes change can seem impossible. The prospect of living differently can feel unrealistic and overwhelming. Discouragement takes root, and we begin to discount the idea before we even get started. When failure in the past has prevailed, it's hard to remain positive about trying again.

Deciding to do a new thing starts with the decision to try again. But this time we do it with the positivity of hope. Change requires at least a glimmer of hope that healing is possible. Can you muster up a little hope? Can you at least open the window a crack to let a whisper of hope squeeze in? Just say yes. All God needs to make things change is your decision to allow hope to spark. It comes down to choosing to hope.

Hope makes us feel expectant and desire what is good. It is what the love of God holds for us as shown in 1 Corinthians 13:7, "Love never gives up, never loses faith, is always hopeful, and endures through every circumstance." We will hear further about this Scripture next week. For now, we must know that our hope comes from love, and that is where God comes in.

Where does hope come from? How do we find it? Let's see what Scripture says about the source of true hope.

"And now, Lord, what do I wait for? My hope is in you?" (Psalm 39:7 NKJV)
"You will show me the path of life; In Your presence is fullness of joy; at your right hand are pleasures forevermore." (Psalm 16:11 NKJV)

In Psalm 39:7, David was talking to himself and asking the Lord at the same time, "Why am I waiting? You, Lord, are where my hope comes from. What am I waiting for?" Psalm 16:11 spells out plainly where we find the path to a life with fullness of joy and pleasures forevermore; it is in the presence of God. This kind of life is not just fulfilled when we arrive in heaven but is a path of life achievable right now. By acceptance of God's son, Jesus, we are spiritually allowed in the presence of God here and now. Our spirit can be reconnected to God's; hope can be restored. Your hope is in God.

You might ask how hope in God can help change your circumstances. Let me show you what Jesus said about it.

"Jesus looked at them and said, 'With man this is impossible, but with God all things are possible.'" (Matthew 19:26)

"If you can?" said Jesus, "Everything is possible for one who believes." (Mark 9:23)

"He replied, 'Because you have so little faith. Truly I tell you, if you have faith as small as a mustard seed, you will say to this mountain, "Move from here to there," and it will move. Nothing will be impossible for you.'" (Matthew 17:20)

Jesus wants us to have hope at least the size of a mustard seed, because he can move a mountain with a minuscule amount of faith. Anything is possible with the power of God. When we begin to hope, belief can take root. And if we have belief, God can create change in our life.

The first step to change is having hope in God. With a tiny seed of faith from us, God can remove ancient, imbedded boulders from our life.

Chains of struggle we have resigned to carry with us to our grave can be broken and discarded.

Past hurts can stop hurting us.

Devastating memories can stop being played over and over in our dreams and reality.

Crushing pain of a traumatic childhood can be resolved.

Peace can reign.

Freedom can be won with the power of Christ.

In order to look to God as our hope, we must enter into a relationship with him. And, as with any relationship and commitment, we must go in with our eyes open and with a clear understanding of what we're getting into. So, before we go any further and make any commitment, we need to settle a few misconceptions so we can walk into hope with correct thinking.

We Are Not Born Good

The first misconception we need to tackle is the idea that we are born good. When we are born, we enter the world as a sinner. Society challenges the theory of original sin. Instead, many people have come to believe we are inherently good from birth and the exposure of our experiences creates bad in us. According to the Bible, this is false thinking and opposite of the truth. Deciding to change takes a conscious choice to commit all of our life to Jesus Christ, because without Christ, we are dead in our sin.

The truth is we are not born good. The environment isn't what turns us bad; we are born with rebellion in our hearts. We are born with the corruption of sin in our nature. It causes us to be self-absorbed and seek things we want instead of following God's instruction.

Take a one-year-old child that has just started walking. He begins exploring his surroundings with no regard to his own personal safety or the thought of right versus wrong. The child is told *no* repeatedly by his parents, in an effort to teach him boundaries and keep him safe. Soon, he knows not to touch that shiny object because Mom and Dad have said no every time he reaches his hand towards it. But if you turn your head, what will he do? He will deliberately turn to touch what he has been repeatedly warned not to touch. It's in our nature to be rebellious and self-serving. It's in that small child's nature to want his own way, even if it's at the cost of rebellion to his parents. We are sinners in need of God's restoration from the time we are born.

Paul says it plainly in Romans:

> *"For all have sinned and fall short of the glory of God."* (3:23)

All have sinned. Every one of us falls short when compared to a faultless God who carries no sin in his nature.

Here's another example for you. An infant, so sweet-smelling and tiny, enters the world and is immediately on a journey to get her own way. At first she cries to tell you she needs food or a diaper change. Soon she cries because she wants her way.

"Pick me up!" Nothing's wrong; she's dry, safe, fed, healthy, and loved. In fact, you have held her so much she has decided being put down is unacceptable. She now uses her cries to get you to pick her up.

Don't believe me? Think a baby could never be bad? Then why does that baby arch its back and struggle away from you? That, my friend, is rebellion. It's a child wanting its own way, which is rebellion and comes from our sin nature. We are born with a nature that pushes us toward self-satisfaction and sin.

If left alone with no outside influence, will a child do what's good? Or will it hit other children, take the toy it wants, and get mad because it wants its own way? I think you know the answers. No, we are not born good; this much is clear.

There Is a Penalty for the Fall of Man

Here's our second misconception. Society teaches us that we came from the evolution of an ape instead of a work of art created by God. Don't even get me started about evolution. If every animal evolved from another, then where are all the fossils? Not one transitional fossil exists that would prove the existence of those wonky, half-and-half animals. When hundreds of thousands of animals exist, not one fossil showing an animal transitioning? I could go on, but let's get back to the fall of man.

According to Genesis, God created everything, including Adam and Eve. Who then decided to disobey the one rule God gave them? They ate a piece of fruit that left a curse on mankind and caused our original sin. It caused us all to carry sin in our nature.

Have you heard of "cause and effect"? A certain action will cause an equal and opposite reaction in return. Every action has a reaction; a consequence. The action of disobedience by Adam and Eve had consequences—not just for Adam and Eve but for all of us. The penalty of sin has been passed down to every generation since.

Sin is unholy and comes from evil, and God is the opposite of sin. Therefore sin carries a hefty consequence. There is a price to be paid for every crime committed. You wouldn't commit a crime, go to court, and expect there to be no penalty assessed and dispensed. Justice demands payment when we commit a crime, just as sin also demands payment.

"For the wages of sin is death, but the gift of God is eternal life in Christ Jesus our Lord."
(Romans 6:23)

God would rather that Adam and Eve had not disobeyed, eaten the fruit, and been subject to the penalty that their actions carried. But their choice tied his hands.

The consequence of their decision invoked the penalty of death. It couldn't be escaped, if God is a just God.

That means, if we are all sinners because of the nature we are born with, we are doomed the minute we are born. From the moment we leave the womb we are guilty before God of the crime of "sin." When we come to the age where we understand this, we are accountable for our sin. If God is a good and just judge, he must punish the crime with the appropriate penalty—death. Meaning we are condemned to hell, eternal death, because of our sin nature.

Maybe you're saying, "But God is love and he is forgiving." True, but his character is not just love. It's much more. Part of his character is also justice. So while he wants to forgive everyone for the sin nature they are born with, he must be true to his nature and uphold righteousness. He is a just God.

When you are of legal age deemed accountable for your actions in a criminal court, you stand before a judge and receive a just and accurate penalty for the crime you have committed. At least you would expect to get the accurate penalty assessed for your crime, if the judge was good and not corrupt. You wouldn't want to stand before a corrupt judge dispensing justice unfairly and incorrectly. A corrupt judge couldn't be trusted; you might get a wrong sentence. You might think it okay if you got a lighter sentence, but what if you got a heavier one?

A just judge is a good judge, and God is a good judge. He can be nothing less.

The penalty of sin is death, and it's something all mankind is condemned by from the moment of birth. To ignore our condition is to condemn ourselves to eternal death.

Making Jesus Your Personal Savior—Your Bridge to God

Let's make it more personal. Before you can hope in God and have the power to stay committed, you need to enter into a relationship with Jesus Christ and be born again. Jesus is the bridge God provided to cover our original sin. It's like we are in the court room, guilty of our sin, ready for the judge to bang the gavel and give us our penalty. Death for the crime of sin. But as we are standing there waiting, Jesus walks in and says, "I'll pay that penalty for her. I'll take her penalty and die for her. Let her go free." Jesus died and took our penalty of death for us. We can accept the sacrifice he made for us, ask him to enter our life, and begin a relationship with him as our personal savior.

If you have not given your life to Christ, been born again, and received salvation, I'd like to give you that opportunity now.

Steps to Salvation

1. Understand that you are a sinner with no way to pay the penalty of death on your own.
2. Believe that Jesus Christ died on the cross to pay for your sins, and he was resurrected on the third day.
3. Tell Jesus Christ you understand your condition before God and believe he died for your sins so you can be born again.
4. Repent ("turn" from your old life of sin) and follow Jesus Christ and his teaching.
5. Make Jesus Christ the "Lord" (boss) of your life. Do what he says in the Bible.

You can do this through prayer. There's no perfect prayer you have to pray. There's only you telling Jesus that you believe he died for your sins and you want his help. If this is something you need to do, I urge you not to wait. Do it now. Today is the day to make the commitment.

If you would like a little help, I have included a prayer to use as a guideline.

Heavenly Father,

I understand my condition; that I am a sinner and have no way to pay the penalty of death on my own. I believe that you sent your son Jesus Christ to take my place and die on the cross for my sins. I believe that Jesus rose on the third day and overcame death. I now turn from my old life of sin and will follow Jesus Christ and his teachings. I confess now, Jesus to be my personal savior and the Lord of my life. I want to make Jesus the boss of my life.

Amen

If you have just committed your life to Jesus Christ, then half the battle is already won! You have power available others do not have. Committing your will and actions to him is not always easy. It takes daily commitment. You get up every day and commit to follow God's plan and not your own. I understand it's not always easy. Just because we have committed our life to follow Jesus Christ doesn't mean everything in our life is now perfect. It just means we have someone with us who can give us the power to change.

A Decision to Change

Today we are making the decision to change no matter what. No matter how hard it may be or what we may have to give up, overcome, or start doing, we are going to draw a line in the sand and not cross back over.

Today is the day we say, *Yes. We will do what it takes!* Knowing that we are not doing it alone. Today, we commit to ourselves to stay *until*. To keep going *until*. To keep getting back up when we fall down. To keep going, keep trying, keep hoping, and keep believing.

I have struggled with getting back up when I fall down. Failure is hard. I start out committed and strong, only to stumble, fall down, and stay down while I berate myself and lick my wounds. I have to admit, my failures can send me into a mental downward spiral that leads me to think, "What's the use?" The voices in my head scream loudest when I'm down. Those are the voices that make me want to stop trying. *But those thoughts are not God's voice.* They are my mental thought processes, and they need to change.

So here's help to grasp onto. Stay connected to Jesus and keep looking up. Say *no* to the voice inside you saying "What's the use? Just give up." Talk back to the voices inside you.

When you look to Jesus and ask him to help, you can get back up. Instead of believing the lies circling in your head, you have to stop yourself, put handcuffs on that thought, and go to the One who can change things. We can have all kinds of mental understanding, but power comes from talking directly to Jesus. Go to God in prayer and say, "Help me. Help me see the truth about this situation. Help me keep going. Give me the strength and understanding I don't have." If you can do nothing else, just cry out and say, "HELP!"

Deciding to change isn't easy. Committing to stay *until* is even harder. Everything in you will tell you to stop, but you have to keep going. Commitment to change means you have to be unmovable about your decision. You have to say, "Nothing and no one will stop me!" and mean it with everything you've got. Then when you feel like stopping, you ask for help.

Starting today, each morning when you get up is a new day to recommit. Start your morning tomorrow by giving your day to what God has for you and see how it changes the way you live and think.

Hope is on your side. You are newly created. You've got this. Scripture says God finishes whatever he starts (Philippians 1:6), and he has started something new in you. Let Jesus's power rise up in you and change your life. You are more capable than you have ever been with Christ as your advocate.

"And I am certain that God, who began the good work within you, will continue his work until it is finally finished on the day when Christ Jesus returns." (Philippians 1:6)

SESSION FOUR REFLECTION QUESTIONS

Has there been a point in your life where it was easier to just stay where you were? Are you there right now? Explain.

What does it mean for you to have hope in God?

Explain how a judge is considered good?

Explain what it meant for mankind when God sent Jesus as a substitute.

What does it mean to be a sinner with no way to pay the penalty of death?

In your own words explain what salvation means.

Have you made the commitment to Jesus Christ? If so, when and where? If not, why not?

What stops you from succeeding to make changes in your life?

If all things are possible with God, what do you need to be possible right now? Honestly explain what you need help changing.

Put your commitment to change in writing and sign it like a contract to yourself.

SESSION FIVE

Learning to Trust God

Now that we have established God is big enough, he cares enough to help, and we've committed ourselves to change, it's time to learn to trust. You have to take a leap of faith and put your trust out there. You have to decide God is who he says he is, and he did what he said he did, concerning Jesus Christ.

Trust is a small word with big implications. The definition of trust is:

Trust—firm belief or confidence in the honesty, integrity, reliability, justice of another person or thing. Faith. Reliance.[1]

It takes faith to trust God. It takes putting aside all your preconceived notions and deciding to take the Bible for what it says as truth. Trust doesn't always come easy. Maybe you're an analytical thinker. Or maybe your experiences have shown you that trusting is a high-risk endeavor.

Can I ask you something? Would you be willing to put aside your past and look at the topic of trust with fresh eyes? Can you approach the topic with an open mind and look at it with a new prospective? Take all your experiences and decisions not to trust and put them on the floor next to you just for this lesson. If you still want to pick them up when we're done, you are welcome to do so. But for this lesson, can you open your heart and look at trusting God with an unbiased view?

We All Have a Picture of God in Our Mind

Our picture of God often looks like our most dominant parental figure, which is usually our father. Maybe you had a father who was cruel, angry, absent, distant, or unavailable. Possibly, you had a great father who was loving and kind. If you look closely at your idea of who God is, it will probably be close to the characteristics of your own father.

If your father was loving, available, kind, and encouraging, it's easier to see God in that way. However, if your father was a harsh disciplinarian task-master, you will tend to think of God as harsh. In your mind he is waiting for you to mess up so he can smack your hands.

But God isn't like man. He doesn't carry the sin nature we do. God isn't distant, absent, or unavailable. He isn't angry and cruel. He isn't impatient or quick to criticize.

He doesn't forget about his children and family. He doesn't make promises he doesn't keep. He doesn't carry the flaws that man does.

Think about it. Have you looked at God wrong because of the image your parents cast?

Trusting God Has to Be Based on His Character, Not Man's

It's not uncommon for someone to struggle with trust when they have been hurt by the people entrusted with their wellbeing. If your parents were supposed to take care of and protect you, and instead caused you harm, trust becomes difficult. It only makes sense. If you couldn't trust those who were supposed to love you here on earth, how can you trust a God who's unseen?

Maybe your injured heart comes from someone other than your parents. Instead your pain comes from family, friends, children, or a spouse who have failed you. Whoever caused you to doubt the trustworthiness of God, their image pales in comparison to who God really is.

Unlike the people who have failed you, God doesn't have a flawed character. He is trustworthy because of who he is. When we begin to see God's character clearly and can separate it from man's character, trusting him becomes much easier.

Let's prove it by taking a look at elements of God's character. If we can be assured God has a trustworthy character, maybe we can step out in faith and trust him to help us.

All good things take some risk, but placing trust in things or people unworthy of our trust is a bad idea. Calculated risk can bring huge reward. However, stepping into a risky situation without doing the calculation is just plain foolish. Any risk you take should be evaluated against the payoff. Does the reward greatly outweigh the amount of risk you are taking?

When you begin to understand that God is a God of integrity, his character makes it impossible for him to do anything other than good. The risk, then, becomes miniscule in comparison to the rewards you receive. The payoff to trusting God is big.

The Character of God

The first, and I believe the greatest, attribute of God is love. Let's start here.

God is Love.

"Whoever does not love does not know God, because God is love." (1 John 4:8)

The Greek word for "love" used here and many other places in the New Testament is *agape*. It's used here as a noun, a person. It means God-love. A supremely self-sacrificing love that can only be described as God himself.

God is love and carries all the characteristics of love. He is all 1 Corinthians 13:4–8 shows love to be.

"Love is patient, love is kind. It does not envy, it does not boast, it is not proud. It is not rude, it is not self-seeking, it is not easily angered, it keeps no record of wrongs. Love does not delight in evil but rejoices with the truth. It always protects, always trusts, always hopes, always perseveres. Love never fails."

Here's what this Scripture says God is like:

God is patient—He is able to accept, tolerate, and suffer through our delays and problems without becoming annoyed or anxious.

God is kind—His nature is to show friendliness, generosity, and to be considerate.

God doesn't envy or boast—He doesn't resentfully long for the qualities or possessions of others. He doesn't talk with excessive pride about his achievements and abilities.

God is not proud—He doesn't have an excessively high opinion of his importance. He just is who he is.

God is not rude or self-seeking—He is not offensively impolite or ill-mannered.

God is slow to get angry—He is long-suffering with us and is slow to feel strong annoyance, displeasure, or hostility towards our failures.

God doesn't keep track of what we do wrong—there is no score sheet holding all our wrongs against us. He forgives and chooses to forget our wrongs.

God doesn't delight in our evil but rejoices with the truth—Truth is always his way. He takes no joy out of our failures. The minute we repent and turn to truth, he rejoices.

God always protects us—He is always trying to keep us safe from harm or injury.

God always trusts us—He believes in us, in our abilities, strengths, and reliability.

God always hopes for us—He feels expectant and desires for our good.

God always perseveres because he's faithful—He is loyal, constant, and steadfast.

God never fails—He is never unsuccessful in achieving his goals.

If God is love, then to be filled with love, we must be filled with God. We need to be completely surrendered to him, so he can fill us with himself.

God is Light.

"This is the message we have heard from him and declare to you; God is light; in Him there is no darkness at all." (1 John 1:5)

God is light. We are told to walk in his light. What does it mean to walk in the light he embodies? We may never completely understand the light of God; our sin nature precludes us from it. Fathoming his full glory escapes us. But the term *light* does give us a comprehensible picture which helps us come to a clearer understanding.

Light is often referred to as goodness versus darkness connoting evil. Light shines, helps us see, and causes growth. It illuminates our surroundings and helps us to see what direction we are going. With light we can avoid stumbling around in the dark, risking bodily harm and even death. Light brings with it photosynthesis, the chemical energy converted from light energy used by plants cells to grow. All living creatures, including humans, require light to grow and be healthy.

God is the light shining on us. He illuminates our surroundings and helps us see where we are going. In his light, we can grow strong, like a great oak tree with deep roots. When fully mature, a great oak tree provides shade of its own. It can reproduce itself by dropping seeds, and it helps provide oxygen for humans to breath.

When God provides the light of himself, we grow in him and become like a mature, great oak tree. Eventually, we provide shade by offering a shoulder or a kind word when someone is struggling. We reproduce ourselves by sharing all God has done in our own life. Other travelers along our path begin to breathe clean air when we point the lost, lonely, and afraid to God's light.

God is Holy.

"But just as he who called you is holy, so be holy in all you do." (1 Peter 1:15)

Holy by definition in the Greek language is *hagios,* meaning separated from sin, pure, blameless, perfect consecrated.[2]

Holy means all good, all the time. No sin or deviation from goodness can occur in God. It cannot be; it cannot happen. Because of his character of holiness, he is incapable of error, evil, or sin. He is pure and perfect with "good" being who he is.

If God cannot be anything but good, then the angry-God-up-in-the-sky theory is blown out of the water. It also dispels the assumption that God is distant and uncaring. If God is truly good and loving, he has to also be caring and kind.

I love the verses in Isaiah 6:1–3 (NKJV). It says this:

"In the year that King Uzziah died, I saw the Lord sitting on the throne, high and lifted up, and the train of His robe filled the temple. Above it stood seraphim; each one had six wings; with two he covered his face, with two he covered his feet, and with two he flew. And one cried to another and said: 'Holy, holy, holy, is the Lord of hosts; the whole earth is full of His glory!'"

The prophet Isaiah got a glimpse of the glory of God in his vision. *Holy, Holy, Holy! … The whole earth is full of His glory!* Picture it. The seraphim around the throne are so filled with euphoria, words of adoration spill out of their mouths over and over. The glory of God is so expansive that they are enraptured by it. It would be impossible to close their mouths and stop praising God. They can't help themselves; they are involuntarily compelled to praise.

Imagine it. The throne of the Lord, high and lifted up, as if floating on the clouds. The train of his robe draped through the entire temple, never-ending, white, illuminated linen, flowing and flowing, softest cloth ever felt to the touch. Majestic beings surrounding the throne, so beautiful your breath catches in your throat just looking at them. And they are so enraptured by the glory they find themselves in that they are induced to praise. The picture is so breathtakingly spectacular you need to remind yourself to breath.

Have you ever been so full of excitement it was impossible to keep composed? I imagine it to be times a thousand in the presence of a holy, glory-filled God. His glory, I'm sure, is astonishingly awe-inspiring, but his goodness is far beyond what we could ever understand. And it comes from his character of holiness.

God is Omnipresent.

"Where can I go from Your Spirit? Where can I flee from your presence? If I go up to the heavens, you are there; if I make my bed in the depths, you are there. If I rise on the wings of the dawn, if I settle on the far side of the sea, even there your hand will guide me, your strength, your right hand will hold me fast." (Psalm 139:7–10)

Omnipresent is just a big word meaning he is all-present. In other words, he exists everywhere. There is no place God is not. Naively, we think we can hide things from God's sight, but he sees it all. Even trying to hide in hell is a futile effort. He is there too. He is in all places at once.

The Psalmist asks, *"Where can I go from your Spirit?"* He asks because the Spirit of God is everywhere. God is not absent from where you are. The attempt to hide your life and circumstances from God is futile. Believing you can do anything without him seeing your actions is a shallow lie. Clearly, Scripture teaches God is present in our world and lives. You can try to run from him but there is no place to go where he isn't present.

God is Omnipotent.

"Holy, holy, holy is the Lord God Almighty, who was and is, and is to come." (Revelation 4:8b)

Omnipotent, another big word that simply means all-powerful. He is almighty, all-powerful, and ever-existent. Always was, is right now, and always will be.

"And I heard, as it were, the voice of a great multitude, as the sound of many waters and as the sound of mighty thundering's, saying, 'Alleluia! For our Lord God Omnipotent reigns!'" (Revelation 19:6 NKJV)

The Lord God all-powerfully reigns! We do not have to feel intimidated by the power of darkness or this world. Nothing is beyond the power of God. He owns all the power and isn't reluctant to use it for the good of his people. In Revelation 19, we see a tremendous crowd, a great multitude of people. John describes the sound of all those voices as many waters and mighty thundering. He doesn't say *or*; he says *and*.

He describes both sounds of rushing water and loud peals of thunder, trying to accurately display the deafening sound with which the multitude shouted. Picture in your mind's eye, white water rapids rushing and thunder clapping simultaneously. Eardrum-bursting roaring might more accurately describe the level of sound.

The picture he is trying to paint for us concerning the level of noise is actually people speaking. They were all making the same statement in unison: "Alleluia! For the Lord God Omnipotent reigns!"

Alleluia is the Greek form of the word *Hallelujah* meaning, "Praise ye Jah! An adoring exclamation of Praise You Jehovah!"[3]

A crowd amassed and thundered with a deafening unified voice, saying "Praise You Jehovah! For you are powerful and you reign over everything!"

God is Faithful.

> "Therefore know that the Lord your God, He is God, the faithful God who keeps covenant and mercy for a thousand generations with those who love Him and keep His commandments." (Deuteronomy 7:9 NKJV)

Faithful—maintaining allegiance, constant, loyal. Marked by a showing of strong sense of duty or responsibility.[4]

God's allegiance doesn't change. He is *constant*. He is unchanging.

Constant. What a great word! It means he does not change; he remains firm in his purpose. He remains steady in his affections or loyalties. God is constant, reliable, and nothing can change him. Circumstances don't change him. He doesn't change when society shifts its direction or belief. What was true a thousand years ago is still true today. You can rely on what he says to remain true. Not just for a thousand years but a thousand generations.

God doesn't forget his commitments or his loyalties. He remains the same no matter the circumstance or the passing of time.

God is Justice.

> "Far be it from you to do such a thing – to kill the righteous with the wicked, treating the righteous and the wicked alike. Far be it from you! Will not the Judge of all the earth do right?" (Genesis 18:25)

To be just means to be guided by truth, reason, justice, and fairness. You might think God is just. He is just because he embodies the quality of justice; it is who he is, not just something he does. He cannot be unjust. He is always guided by the truth. Justice is the quality of being righteous and rectitude. Being impartial and fair. It is the use of authority and power to uphold what is right, just, or lawful.

Justice confronts the moral situation in a man and either justifies or condemns him by his morals. Not because of feelings for the individual but for the judgment of morality.

God is the judge of all the earth. Righteousness and judgment are who he is. God acts justly from within. He is not more or less just depending on the person. He will always act justly.

Unlike us, he does not get caught between justice and mercy. They function together without quarreling. His mercy is made perfect while justice prevails. This is why he provided a way out of original sin. In his mercy, he provided Jesus Christ to pay the penalty of death, and justice was served while we still received mercy.

There are many more attributes of God we could cover, and I encourage you to continue seeking them in the scriptures. But know this: God is trustworthy, dear one. He is fully worth all your trust. Just by the descriptions of his character he can be trusted at his word. There is no way we can completely understand the nature of God. We would need to become gods ourselves to be on his level of understanding. But we don't need full understanding to place our trust in him. His complete nature may be beyond our comprehension, but the knowledge we have is adequate. Step into faith and into his arms. He will provide the rest.

SESSION FIVE REFLECTION QUESTIONS

Do you struggle with trust? If so, why?

Describe how you picture God. Have you pictured God wrongly because of the image your parents cast?

Explain what it means for you to take a calculated risk.

Pick three attributes from 1 Corinthians 13:4–8 that you may have trouble believing. What would it mean for you, if God proved those attributes to be true?

Describe what it means for God to be light. What about God's light do you most need in your life?

Describe the meaning of holiness. What does God's holiness mean for you personally?

Explain what omnipresent means and how it affects you personally.

Explain what omnipotent means and how it affects you personally.

Explain what God's faithfulness means and how it affects you personally.

Explain what the attribute of justice means and how it affects you personally.

After seeing the true character of God this week, how do you now feel about trusting God?

SESSION SIX

Understanding Where We Came From

Core beliefs are what make us think the way we do. How you grew up and what you learned from previous generations continue in you, creating your belief system. The issue is that our *behavior* (actions) comes from our *thinking* which comes from our *beliefs*. And if our beliefs are wrong, then we act from faulty thinking.

This lesson will focus on how our childhood impacts our behavior and how God's truth contrasts with our wrong beliefs. First, we'll look at why our past is important, and how drama continues in our life from generation to generation. Second, we will see how God's truth then responds to where we came from, changing where we go when we change what we believe. This is an important truth that will help identify false core beliefs. Once we identify false beliefs, we can then change how we think, and more positive actions will follow.

Our Yesterday Is Important

If wholeness is the goal for current, day-to-day life, why look at the past? Why drag up all the trauma and pain from yesterday? Because when it comes to emotional issues, productively living in the present is difficult when you haven't honestly dealt with your past. A painful yesterday is important to resolve because it doesn't stay in yesterday. It creeps into our present and affects the way we think and act today.

According to author David Seamands in his book, *Healing for Damaged Emotions*, there are four types of pain from our past: hurts, humiliations, hates, and horrors. Hurts are caused from rejection and abandonment. Humiliations show up from embarrassments, shame, unworthiness, inadequacy, and inferiority. Hates stick with us from resentments, bitterness, unforgiveness, anger, and rage. Horrors stay with us from fears, anxiety, and terrors. All four types of pain, if not healed, will carry forward and direct how you live and view life.[1] Therefore, yesterday cannot stay behind you; it must be healed in order for you to find wholeness in the present.

Dragging Our Excess Baggage into Today

We've talked about baggage before, and how it can really weigh you down in life. Have you ever packed way too much for a trip? At the airport, the excess weight of your baggage puts it over the limit and costs extra. You get to your destination, wear only a third of what you brought, then you buy more stuff, which also needs to return home with you. Of course, this takes additional space in your baggage, which adds more weight and costs more money. This has certainly happened to me. In fact, it's been my story more than once.

My worst baggage story was from a business trip I took to New York. Staying only one night didn't stop me from packing enough for a week. Bad enough that my bag had unneeded weight, but add to it the style of the bag, a hanging one with only a shoulder strap to carry it. All our appointments were traveled to on foot. And leaving directly for the airport from our last appointment of the day meant carrying my shoulder-strap baggage everywhere while wearing a business suit and high heel shoes. By the time we arrived at the first appointment, both my shoulders, my back, and my feet hurt so bad I had a horrible time focusing. The next trip I took to New York I changed everything: I packed light, wore flat shoes, and bought luggage with wheels. I learned that lugging excess baggage around was painful.

Just as I slung around excess baggage in New York, we often tote along excess luggage on our trip through life. We start out in childhood and adolescence collecting baggage, then move it with us into adulthood. We hang onto way too much of the excess baggage of our childhood. When we are supposed to move out of childhood and become adults, we instead continue to live through the lens and pain of the past. Apostle Paul said this:

"When I was a child, I spoke as a child, I understood as a child, I thought as a child; but when I became a man, I put away childish things." (1 Corinthians 13:11 NKVJ)

Instead of putting away childish things, though, we often carry them with us on our voyage through life. They hinder our progress of becoming an adult. We stay a child emotionally. We react in childish ways. We learn to parent ourselves the same way we were parented in childhood. We become stunted emotionally, and instead of behaving in a mature fashion, we react with the same coping mechanisms we learned in childhood.

Have you ever thought to yourself after saying or doing a particular thing, "That was stupid. That was a childish thing to do"? How did you feel about your action? Did you have a positive feeling? Did you become critical of yourself for having the thought or feeling? Did you ask yourself, "Where in the world did that come from?" Just like the excess baggage on my trip, these childish things are baggage you drag around from the past.

The Life Drama Triangle

Dysfunction in the family, which none of us are immune from experiencing, may cause us to continue in life on what Stephen Karpman M.D. calls *The Life Drama Triangle*.[2]

The Life Drama Triangle is a model of social interaction involving three roles people unconsciously play or try to manipulate other people to play. Many interactive situations end up as triangle interactions, with the result of people feeling bad about each other and themselves. We can find triangle transactions occurring in less extreme degrees in our daily interactions with others. At times, we even engage in triangle transactions with ourselves, through self-talk.

According to Webster's Dictionary, a defense mechanism in psychiatry terms is any thought process, such as repression, introjection, or sublimation, unconsciously used by an individual as a defense against feelings of guilt, anxiety, or shame.[3]

In simple layman's language, defense mechanisms are the ways we protect ourselves from things we don't want to think about or deal with. It's how we distance ourselves from a full awareness of unpleasant thoughts, feelings, and behaviors. In the operation of the Life Drama Triangle, the defense mechanism known as "denial" is at play.

Denial takes on four forms:

To protect our actions or the actions of another person, we use denial to excuse ourselves by denying: the fact that it ever happened, our awareness there was a problem, the impact our actions have on others, or that we have any responsibility. We can be in denial in one or more forms and even move in and out of different forms.

Denial of fact:	"It didn't happen."
Denial of awareness:	"It may have happened, but I didn't know it happened because…"
Denial of impact:	"It happened, but it didn't hurt anybody."
Denial of responsibility:	"It happened, but it happened because of some external factor, some mistake, or because of some provocation by the victim."

LIFE DRAMA TRIANGLE

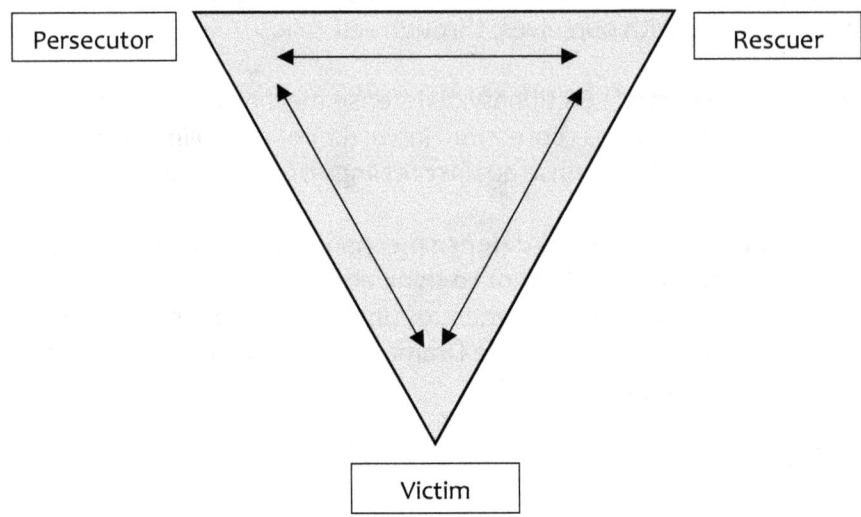

The three triangle roles are:

* **Persecutor.** The persecutor has the stance of, "It's all your fault!" They criticize and blame the victim, set strict limits, can be rigid, controlling, angry, and authoritative. The victim is kept feeling oppressed by the persecutor's bullying and threats. The persecutor can't be flexible, bend, or be vulnerable for fear of the risk of becoming a victim themselves. They yell, criticize, and bully, but don't actually solve any problems.

  The extreme version of this person becomes a perpetrator on their victim in the role of verbal, physical, emotional, or sexual abuse. They have all the power in an interaction, yet take none of the responsibility.

* **Victim.** The victim has the stance of "poor me!" Victims have none of the power in the interaction yet typically take all of the responsibility. Victims see themselves as victimized, oppressed, powerless, helpless, dejected, and ashamed. They come across as super sensitive.

  A person in the victim role has real difficulties making decisions, solving problems, finding pleasure in life, or understanding their self-perpetuating behaviors. They look for a rescuer, a savior, to save them. If someone refuses or fails to do that, they can quickly perceive them now as a persecutor.

The extreme version of this person plays the role of the recipient of abuse either verbally, physically, emotionally, or sexually.

* **Rescuer.** The stand of the rescuer is, "Let me help you!" This person works hard to help and take care of other people. They need to rescue other people to feel good about themselves, while neglecting their own needs or not taking responsibility for meeting their own needs. The rescuer is classically an enabler and co-dependent, needing to help. They often can't allow the victim to get better or succeed and use guilt to keep the victim dependent. They are frequently overworked, harried, tired, and live like a martyr while resentment festers underneath.

    The extreme version of this person in the cycle of abuse becomes a silent partner. They may or may not know the abuse is taking place. They have the potential to rescue the victim, yet because of their approach to power and responsibility, they end up rescuing the perpetrator. A silent partner operates out of fear and ignorance.[4]

Notes about the Life Drama Triangle:

* Each role on the triangle has a payoff. Victims feel taken care of, rescuers feel good by being a caretaker, and persecutors get to feel superior to the victim and rescuer.

* The cost of staying on the triangle is high. The costs are perpetuating a dysfunctional social dynamic and missing out on the possibility of healthy, resonant, resilient relationships.

* You can change roles on the triangle. In fact, everyone is locked into playing one of the three roles or moving back and forth between them for a lifetime unless they get off.

* You can perpetrate against yourself. Self-abuse and self-hate are just two examples of perpetrating against yourself. Cutting is a common form of self-abuse.

* To get off the triangle, you first have to tell the truth about where you are and feel the feelings. Own and take responsibility for where you are on the drama triangle. Then place your life and future in the hands of Jesus Christ and begin the process of change.

* When the victim moves off the triangle, they are seen as perpetrators by both the silent partner (rescuer) and the perpetrator. Any time the victim moves off the triangle, those playing other roles on the triangle will not

be pleased. The balance of abuse has been disrupted. Those playing other roles do not want to face their own problems and will shift blame.

The first step off the triangle is to be aware of what's happening, how it works, and what roles you play most frequently. What role did you play as a child? What roles did others in your family play? Are you or they still playing them?

Once you've become aware of the patterns, it becomes much easier to recognize when it is happening and step out of it. Live with integrity; you are responsible for being 100 percent honest, both with yourself and with others. This means acknowledging and honoring your own feelings and needs, and allowing others to be responsible for theirs. It also means taking responsibility for your own actions and consequences, and letting others do the same. This might require some "tough love," both toward yourself and others.

The Sins of Our Ancestors

According to Scripture, in Exodus, and again in Deuteronomy, the sins of the father are passed down on the children to the third and fourth generation.

And he passed in front of Moses, proclaiming, "The Lord, the Lord, the compassionate and gracious God, slow to anger, abounding in love and faithfulness, maintaining love to thousands, and forgiving wickedness, rebellion and sin. Yet he does not leave the guilty unpunished; he punishes the children and their children for the sins of the fathers to the third and fourth generation." (Exodus 34:6–7)

You shall not make for yourself an idol in the form of anything in heaven above or on the earth beneath or in the waters below. You shall not bow down to them or worship them; for I, the Lord your God, am a jealous God, punishing the children for the sin of the fathers to the third and fourth generation of those who hate me, but showing love to thousands who love me and keep my commandments. (Deuteronomy 5:8–10)

But in other scriptures, we see that the father is not responsible for the sins of the son and vice versa.

Yet he did not put the sons of the assassins to death, in accordance with what is written in the Book of the Law of Moses where the Lord commanded; "Fathers shall not be put to death for their children, nor the children put to death for their fathers; each is to die for his own sins." (2 Kings 14:6)

The soul who sins is the one who will die. The son will not share the guilt of the father, nor will the father share the guilt of the son. The righteousness of the righteous man will be credited to him, and the wickedness of the wicked will be charged against him. (Ezekiel 18:20)

So how does it work? Do the sins get carried down from generation to generation or not? Are we doomed to repeat the sins of our fathers?

What God is trying to tell us is this: *sin is passed down from generation to generation, if we remain outside of him.* In Deuteronomy 5:8–10, there is a key point. It says "of those who hate me." The generations to come who experience the penalty of the father's sins are "those who hate God."

In John 14:15, Jesus said, "If you love me, you will obey what I command." When we choose to live life on our own, what we are saying is we love our own ways, not God and his ways. We put ourselves on the throne and live for ourselves instead of God. If we love God, we obey his commands he has given us in the Bible. If we choose not to love God, we make ourselves as the idol in our life. God sees our choice as idol worship. You cannot worship God and yourself; it's one or the other. In the instance of worshipping self, you are separated from God and his protection. The sin of past generations is then able to pass down to you.

Sins of the Father Become Sins of the Children

The sins of the father are continued in the children as they become the sins of the children. It is not your father's sins or the past generations' sins you are accountable to God for, but your own sins. When you choose to do the same sins that are passed down from the previous generation, you are held accountable for your actions. But because of God's grace, the children can confess their own sins and the sins of their fathers and be forgiven and accepted by God. (Leviticus 26:40–42)

God does not arbitrarily impose all your sins on your children. The Bible says, "The son is not accountable for the sins of the father, and the father is not accountable for the sins of the son."

The principle is this: By the example of the parents, there is a strong possibility that the children will follow the example set and sin in the same way.

Children repeat what they see in their parents because we learn most effectively by the example we are shown. Parents have the greatest influence of anyone in the life of a child. Children begin by mimicking your words and movements. They pick up your attitudes, actions, and beliefs. If you are in rebellion against God, your children will likely follow suit.

We are affected by one hundred years before us, which is three to four generations, and what we do will affect one hundred years after us, another three to four generations. Amazing, isn't it?

I remember one time looking up at my own son at the age of nine as he stood before me; legs spread apart, hand on his hip, jaw extended, teeth clenched, and face tilted up toward the ceiling. In that moment I experienced déjà vu. I knew exactly where his defiant stance had come from. It was like looking in the mirror. When I was angry and wanted him to know I meant business, I would stand the very same way. He mimicked me perfectly. Point being, children follow what attitudes and behavior they see in their parents. They learn from watching you.

What Choices Will We Make?

Most likely the issues you deal with now began in childhood. Maybe your parents drank and that has also been your issue. It was passed down from the last generation to you. Maybe your father or mother was cruel and angry. Or maybe your parents were neglectful and unplugged. Maybe your problem is stuffing your feelings or feeling inadequate because of a critical parent.

Whatever you are dealing with that has been passed down from previous generations can stop with you. You can begin a new era of emotional and mental health for the generations coming after you. You can leave the next generation with a new way of life and a new legacy.

God's grace, his undeserved favor on us, is poured out on those who love him. When we love him, he provides us with what we need to change ourselves, which in turn will change the future generations in our family. Our destiny is directly tied to the destiny of our children. We must make peace with our past so we can change our destiny and make a future of reconciliation and righteousness for the generations who follow us. There is a lot at stake for us to change.

SESSION SIX REFLECTION QUESTIONS

List one childhood experience for each category below which causes you pain, brings up humiliation, evokes hatred, and sparks horror when you think of it. Why does it still make you feel the same way?

A HURT:

A HUMILIATION:

A HATE:

A HORROR:

Take the above experiences to God in prayer and ask him to change the narrative for your memories. Ask him to remove the hurt, humiliation, hate, and horror from your mind and heart.

Explain what it means to be a perpetrator, victim, and rescuer. Have you ever played any of these roles? If so, explain how.

Have you been using denial as a defense mechanism? Explain.

Do you need to get off the Life Drama Triangle? Begin below with a prayer for help from Jesus.

What wrong behaviors, attitudes, and beliefs did past generations hand down to you?

What will you begin to do to change these wrong behaviors, attitudes, and beliefs? Make a plan.

SESSION SEVEN

Dealing with the Dysfunction of Our Family

In a family with dysfunction, the attention is usually focused on the person who is the most emotionally needy. Often, this person has the component of addiction or compulsive behavior. The attention gets focused on them and the needs of the rest of the family go unmet. Addiction or compulsion may be kept secret, but the children still know something is wrong. They may not be able to pinpoint the exact problem, but at a subconscious level, they know something is wrong.

Occasionally, addiction or compulsion isn't the issue for the emotionally-needy person; instead the person is disabled or living with a long-term physical or mental illness.

Whatever the case, a large portion of everyone's emotional energy revolves around taking care of the needs of the focal family member. In the process, everyone else becomes emotionally needy. Their own emotional needs rarely get met and they become starved for attention.

Other members of the family are rarely allowed to express their feelings when the focus is always placed on an emotionally-needy person. They either stuff their feelings down inside or hide them. Sometimes they are denied altogether. To make emotional pain go away, the person who is denied the ability to express their emotions may find their own ways to medicate themselves.

The message of limiting the expression of feelings may be something spoken or received non-verbally. Things like: "Big boys don't cry," "You're not hurt," "That didn't hurt you," "You're not sad. Be happy," "Quit crying and or I'll give you something to cry about," all give the message, "Don't feel the way you do."

Nonverbal messages can come from a disapproving look or an expression that communicates it's not okay to feel the way you do. Messages may also be communicated when an expression of feelings is just simply ignored because it's not acceptable behavior.

After a child has received the same messages over and over, destructive thoughts develop like, "My feeling are not important. I am not important. My feelings don't matter. I don't have the right to feel pain. I don't have the right to feel."

A child may only be able to feel whatever the needy person feels. "They feel happy so I think I feel happy." A co-dependent relationship is formed and becomes a way of life. In adulthood, they continue to live through the feelings of others, even those outside of the family.

The Code of Silence of an Unhealthy Family

Conflict in a family is normal. Healthy families talk through their conflict and find solutions. In an unhealthy family, a major conflict can occur, and it's swept under the rug like it never happened.

Here's an example to illustrate this. One night, the father comes home in a rage. He screams because there is no dinner waiting for him. His temper escalates towards his wife, calling her horrible names and hitting her across the face. He proceeds to scream and beat her, leaving marks. Dishes fly and shatter. The children, terrified, lock themselves in their bedroom. They think the whole world is coming apart and they fall asleep in the closet afraid. The next day, both the mother and father act as if nothing has happened. Dad drinks coffee at the table while mom prepares lunches for school. They don't talk about it. Everyone knows it happened, but no one mentions it.

This isn't forgiving and forgetting: it' denial. The reality is it happened. Denying reality doesn't make it disappear. It instead creates distrust in the children and teaches them to live in denial themselves. Don't face your problems; deny they exist.

Children learn to play different roles in an emotionally dangerous environment. The role may be chosen by the child or given by the family. It's not done consciously by either. One child may be the scapegoat, the person blamed for all the family's problems, while another is the hero who works hard to bring respect to the family name. The surrogate spouse often takes the place of an emotionally absent spouse. The child then becomes the counselor and confidant for the troubled adult. There is also the invisible one who never gets in the way or causes any trouble.

"*What happens behind closed doors stays behind closed doors*" is the family code of an unhealthy family. The outside world is not allowed to know the family secret. Access to the physical residence may even be limited. Those who do come over see an act, not how the real family behaves. Secrets must stay hidden.

The children learn to protect the needy person in the family. Their job is to keep the secret. They learn to deny the way things are and how they really feel. After engaging in the denial for so long, they may eventually have trouble deciding what is real and recognizing what they feel. Are the feelings their own or do they belong to the needy family member?

Losing Your Childhood

You can lose your childhood three different ways: by becoming a caretaker, through abuse, or by turning off your emotions. Let's explore them one at a time.

Becoming a caretaker. If while still a child, you are thrown into the role of an adult and become someone's caretaker, you lose your own childhood. It can happen for a few reasons: the needy person has an addiction, compulsive behavior, can't function as a responsible adult, is disabled, or suffers with a long-term illness.

If the adults in the family don't take care of the day-to-day emotional and physical needs of the children, someone must do it. A child will often make an unspoken decision to become the caretaker. She tries to be the fixer of people. She smooths out the rough spots in relationships. She becomes the problem solver and covers for her parents when they make mistakes.

Caretakers don't have time to be children. Children were not meant to be the caretaker of the family; they were made to be the ones taken care of.

Abuse. Another way of losing your childhood is from abuse. Abuse can come in many forms: physical, sexual, emotional, spiritual, and verbal.

The ability to trust is established during childhood. When abuse occurs, the child's ability to trust is damaged. When the child is violated by the ones' she is supposed to be able to trust, the message sent is: "Trusting is dangerous. I can't trust anyone." This message is internalized and childhood becomes about survival.

Physical or sexual abuse brings terror into the life of a child. A very big person is acting out behavior on a child who feels small and weak. The abuse brings feelings impossible to express. The child is overwhelmed by the size and authority of the person from whom the abuse comes.
When the abuse is emotional, the child internalizes the punishment and blames herself. Verbal abuse can make a child fearful to answer even the most innocent question. They are constantly on guard for the next attack. Children who are abused put on armor and become "bulletproof." Their innocence has been stolen and with it their childhood is gone. They were thrust into a world of pain and taught to mistrust.

Turning off your emotions. When a traumatic event or a reoccurring emotional trauma happens in a family, the child never has a chance to talk through their feelings. They are not allowed to process the event. These questions are never answered: "What did that mean?" "Why did that happen?" "Are things going to be ok?" The child can go into chronic emotional shock and shut down emotionally.

Healing the Pain of a Lost Childhood

What can be done about reclaiming your childhood? You can't go back and live your life over. You can't go back and be a kid again. You can't change what happened in the past, *but* you can put a new perspective on it. You can find healing for the pain and loss.

When you commit yourself to looking at the past and confronting the pain, you are taking the first step to healing. You have to walk toward the pain not away from it. Confronting the pain of your past is not easy, but remember that healing is on the other side. Don't let your past dominate and control you; instead, begin to take control of your healing.

Let yourself grieve the loss of childhood. The loss is great, and in a way, may feel like a death has occurred. Allow yourself to feel the sadness and loss.

Let the hurt child in you know you understand their pain and they are safe. You may feel like that same little fearful child but you are an adult now. You can even go through the practice of writing your inner child a letter. Tell them you will take care of them now; they can grow up because you are in control and will protect them.

Develop relationships that give you support and emotional warmth. Nurture yourself with kindness that you didn't get as a child. If you missed out on fun, give yourself permission to have fun. Set aside time to do things purely for the enjoyment of them.

If there are positive memories from your childhood, permit yourself to think about them. Be grateful for those times. Allow yourself to remember the good friends, the places you loved to go, a relative who felt safe, or accomplishments that made you feel better about yourself.

Begin to develop healthy, childlike traits. All healthy adults have some childlike traits still with them. Allow yourself to play, laugh, and trust. Be spontaneous and carefree sometimes.

Most of all, let God love you through the process. You are safe with him. You can trust him.

"You did not receive a spirit that make you a slave again to fear, but you received the Spirit of sonship. And by him we cry 'Abba, Father.' The Spirit himself testifies with our spirit that we are God's children. Now if we are children, then we are heirs -

heirs of God and co-heirs with Christ, if indeed we share in his sufferings in order that we may also share in his glory.

I consider that our present sufferings are not worth comparing with the glory that will be revealed in us. The creation waits in eager expectation for the sons of God to be revealed. For the creation was subjected to frustration, not by its own choice, but by the will of the one who subjected it, in hope that the creation itself will be liberated from its bondage to decay and brought into the glorious freedom of the children of God." (Romans 8:15–21)

Getting in Touch with Your Feelings

Are you in touch with what you're feeling? Do you share what you feel with anyone? You need to. Feelings demand expression. Any feelings held inside will eventually find a way out. Either we express them in a healthy way, or they come out in acting out. Sometimes the stuffing of feelings will even make us physically ill.

God gave us our emotions for a reason. They are a gift. They have purpose. Our mind enables us to think, our will to choose, and our emotions should push us to respond. You cannot have good emotions without also experiencing bad ones. Without sorrow there would be no joy; without boredom there would be no excitement; without war there would be no peace. Sharing our emotions builds us up and bonds us in love and friendship.

Just imagine life without emotions. What if you could not feel the pleasure of hanging out with friends, or there were no butterflies in your stomach when the one you love got down on bended knee and proposed? What if there was no feeling of relief upon hearing the diagnosis *all clear*? Or no comfort in a favorite book, your soft bed, or warm soup when you are sick?

Even difficult emotions reflect reality and move us to a better place. They reveal the pain and suffering in our lives. What if you felt no grief or loss after losing a loved one or a friend? Or felt no remorse upon realizing you've hurt someone you love? Even hard emotions give meaning and depth to our lives. When faced head on and processed correctly, they propel us to make a different choice and change our direction.

Whatever you do to try and avoid feelings, continuing on the same path will never get you the emotional health you desire.

Are you intellectualizing your feelings? Trying to keep thoughts and conversations on rational things rather than feeling your feelings? Do you deny your feelings or isolate yourself when you're in emotional pain? Are you trying to deny or control your feelings? How about swallowing your feelings? Do you take a big gulp to swallow what you feel and then do something to try and distract yourself? Maybe you focus on someone else's problems so you don't have to face your own.

Let yourself begin to feel your emotions. Put names to what you are feeling. It's okay to feel sad; to feel angry. Naming your feelings allows you to identify it, put a name to it, and then deal with it.

Find support of some sort and a safe place to let yourself feel. Hearing the stories of others can also help. As you let yourself identify with their story, maybe you will have the courage to share your own. That's what I hope this class helps you do. I hope it gives you courage, tools, and teaches you to push in towards Jesus. Allow him to restore everything in your life, even things with a speck of damage.

I am praying for amazing things to sprout inside you. Even if you can't believe for it yet, I can. I believe enough for us both. God didn't lead you randomly to this study and have me praying for you. He has a plan for you.

SESSION SEVEN REFLECTION QUESTIONS

Was there an emotionally needy person in your family growing up? Explain.

Did your own emotional needs go unmet growing up? Explain.

While growing up, were there limits placed on the expression of feelings? Explain.

Was open talk about problems discouraged in your family? Explain.

Did you play a certain role in your family dynamic that was destructive?

Was talk to the outside world discouraged in your family? Explain.

Did you lose your childhood by becoming a caretaker, by suffering abuse, or turning off your emotions? Explain.

List some ways you will begin to nurture yourself.

Write a letter to the scared little child inside you and tell them you will keep them safe.

How will you begin to develop healthy, childlike traits? List some things you will begin to do.

SESSION EIGHT

Healing Painful Memories

True or false? Time heals all wounds. False. The passing of time doesn't mean healing will occur. In fact, a painful memory left unresolved can actually cause the pain to increase. It has been proven by neuroscientists who study thinking patterns in the brain. Every time a thought is brought forward out of memory, it never goes back the same. It either goes back less or more toxic. Studies also show unresolved toxic memories are brought out in the subconscious during sleep. The brain is trying to clean things up in the thought life.

Painful memories held in our brain cause toxic, negative thinking. They continue to affect the present until you deal with them and find healing. They will drain you spiritually and emotionally. Your energy level is affected. You may not be sure why you feel so drained, but you know something is wrong. The emotional weight of painful memories will take its toll on your physical health.

They may even have a power over you that make you feel stuck. They can make you feel like you are out of control and immobilized with fear. It's like you have no protection from the memories. If the memories overpower you, you may begin to avoid people and situations. If they are strong enough, denying they exist may happen. A lot of energy is needed to live life in denial. You have to constantly reshuffle reality to make it fit your denial system.

Hidden Memories

Some of the most significant memories in our past that were traumatic, hurtful, or humiliating can get locked out of our conscious memory. We can selectively forget. It's as if an emotional circuit breaker is thrown and the terror never happened. When something traumatic happens in a child's life, for example sexual abuse, they are not emotionally equipped to handle the feelings of anger and terror experienced. Often, the feelings are blocked out until they can be properly processed. The process of shutting down intense emotional feelings until they can be processed appropriately can also be seen when someone is grieving. It is a normal part of the grief process when a loved one dies.

After a while the feelings come back. If the child who was sexually abused lives in a severely unhealthy family, it may take years for the trauma to come to the surface so it can be dealt with. The rule of the house is, "We don't talk about it." Instead of working through the feelings, the child will stuff the feelings away. Consciously, the feelings don't exist, but they will cause an undercurrent of emotions that will affect the child their whole life.

When these types of feelings are never processed openly, they can be carried with a person for years and years. Sometimes they remain as an undercurrent for a lifetime. The emotional, physical, and spiritual repercussions are lived with daily by the survivor. How might you know if you have hidden memories deep inside your brain? There are some danger signs you can look for, which I've listed below. See if you identify with any of these scenarios. If so, you may have repressed memories.

> ***Foggy memories of your whole childhood.*** You hear other people talk about their childhood and think to yourself, "I don't remember hardly anything about my childhood." If your childhood was too painful, you may forget large blocks of it.
>
> ***Strange feelings about certain rooms or places in your childhood home.*** When you visualize the house you grew up in, are there rooms that you can't see at all or are unclear, and some you can see clearly? Do some rooms not even exist? When you remember certain rooms, do you feel uneasy or fearful?
>
> ***Inability to feel certain feelings.*** Are you out of touch with your feelings? Do you have one or two main feelings that you are familiar with, like sadness, anger, or depression, but many others are absent?
>
> ***Identifying with stories of others' childhood trauma with no clear reason why.*** As far as you know, no one in your family has an addiction. Your family seems normal with no major trauma you can remember. No one was abused that you remember. In spite of this, you strongly identify with the characteristics of people who have grown up in a traumatic life.

Recognize the Tendencies of People Who Have Had a Traumatic Life

Sometimes after reaching adulthood, we find that what felt normal to us wasn't normal at all. We explore friendships as a teen, begin to see the interactions of other families, and realize they don't have the same dysfunction as our family. As we enter adulthood, we begin to guess at what normal behavior should be. Through the dysfunction in our childhood, we were too busy trying to survive the trauma to learn successful coping strategies. See if you recognize any of these tendencies that people who come from a life of trauma often experience.

> They guess at what normal behavior is.
>
> They feel different from other people.

They are either super-responsible or super-irresponsible.

They lie when it would be just as easy to tell the truth.

They have difficulty with follow-through.

They are hyper-critical of themselves.

They feel like they must be in control.

They are impulsive.

They are often involved in dangerous behaviors.

Recognizing our tendencies is the first step to uncovering repressed memories. Once we recognize them, we can then walk through them with Jesus and learn better coping mechanisms.

Recovering Repressed Memories

Living with repressed memories can be a scary experience. Maybe you're living with night terrors, or only have partial glimpses of the past. Maybe you feel sad, depressed, angry, or fearful when certain things happen but can't reason why. Still, the thought of going into the past and digging around for memories can feel terrifying.

Maybe your first response to the idea of recovering memories is to think, "Why stir things up? I don't really remember, better to leave it alone." I get it. But those repressed memories create bondage in your life even though you don't remember them. To have freedom means remembering, grieving, and allowing Jesus to place new feelings with those memories.

Here are some things you can do to begin to recover any hidden or repressed memories.

Listen to other people's painful stories. Sometimes hearing someone get emotionally involved while describing their painful childhood will start the process of recovering a repressed memory. It also may start by the type of emotion someone expresses. Their emotion may cause you to connect with the same emotion you locked away at the time of your own traumatic experience.

If listening to someone's painful story evokes a deep sadness that you don't understand, this may also be a sign of repressed memories. However, it is not the same as feeling sympathy for another person's loss or tragedy. Feelings of sympathy are understandable and evoke emotions, but this would be a much deeper and more intense reaction to someone's pain.

Ask a relative who is safe. If you begin asking your relatives for information concerning your past, make sure those you approach are safe. Physical and emotional safety is important to move toward health and not additional damage. Talking with someone who has abused you or others in the past may not be a safe person to approach.

If you approach relatives with questions, you need to understand they may be in denial themselves. When the family dynamic is dysfunctional, you need to remember they may feel bound by the same "don't tell" rules that are common to most dysfunctional families. You may not be able to gain any information this way, but it's worth a try.

Make sure you are careful to respect the privacy of your relatives and ask without condemning. Let them know you are not trying to stir up trouble but are working at understanding yourself better.

If you do find a relative to share things with you that you did not know, lost memories may return or incomplete pictures become more complete. Whatever they feel comfortable sharing should be enough for you. Be careful not to push too hard. They may share more at a later date if they feel you handled the information in an appropriate way.

Go visit places from your childhood. Visiting your childhood home may be the spark that lights the flame. Walking through the places where the memories occurred may open the floodgate and begin an emotional journey for you. Just being there in your childhood home may fill in some forgotten memories and unravel the mystery right before your eyes.

Sometimes old friends, their houses, the neighborhood, and places you spent time in will bring back memories. Personally, driving down the street and only seeing the outside of my childhood home brought back some childhood memories for me.

Visit your old schools, the park you may have played at, and other places where you spent time in the neighborhood. As you do, it might be a good idea to jot down notes so you can reflect on them later.

Practice recovery prayer techniques. Repressing memories from a traumatic childhood was a gift from God at the time. Carrying more trauma than we are equipped to handle as a child can cause a serious break from reality. As a child, you were given a way to cope with the trauma until it became time to face it. Through prayer we can begin to ask God to show us the past we can't remember.

Start in prayer by thanking God for being with you. Then ask him to show you any trauma from your childhood that you might be repressing because it was too painful to remember. Ask him to show you what it made you believe about yourself and reveal any lies that you internalized because of it. Finally, ask him to show you what the truth really is about that memory. Allow plenty of time during the process to hear from God. Sit quietly and let him fill you with the answers you need to hear.

Talk with a counselor. Sometimes the pain and memories are buried so deep that the best way to attempt recovery is by talking privately with a counselor. Find a good Christian counselor to help you walk back in time. Getting help takes courage; it is not a sign of weakness.

Healing Painful Memories

The list below are a few ideas to begin the healing process. They are not in order and you do not need to do them as listed. To find healing is individual and these are just suggested ideas. You can do just one or do them all. It's strictly between you and Jesus, what is needed to heal. I would suggest you read through them and begin with what feels most comfortable. Take as much time as needed and let Jesus guide the process.

Tell your story. You take a giant step toward healing when you talk about your pain for the first time. Telling your story takes the power away from it. Evil lives and thrives in the dark. When you bring it into the light, you rob it of its power. Keeping a big secret expends a huge amount of energy. Take back the power it has taken from you. Don't let it drain your energy and spirit any longer. An emotional weight will be lifted, and you will begin to feel freedom from it. Continue talking about your pain. Every time you talk about it in a safe environment, it loses more of its power over you.

When you decide to tell your story, make sure the people you choose to tell are trustworthy. Share with a safe person or group that will give you support and value your courage. A Christian friend, counselor, or support group should consider it a privilege to be there for you.

Feel the emotions. The next element of the journey to bring healing is letting out the emotions you have been holding inside. Some of the emotions you may feel are fear, anger, guilt, and sadness.

As a small child, what you experienced may have felt terrifying. When you begin to face the memories, you may feel fear rise up in you again, like it did as a child. The fear may make you feel scared and unsafe. The terror feels very real, but it can't hurt you any longer. You need to remind yourself the person who hurt you can no longer harm you; you are not the helpless little boy/girl anymore, even though it may feel like it. The pain and fear cannot break you. You are safe now, and God is with you.

Commonly, the following emotion after fear is anger. It's okay to feel the anger. You have to go through the anger to get to the healing. Just make sure you express the anger in an appropriate way that doesn't harm you or anyone else. What happened to you was wrong and you deserve to be angry about it. It's okay to hate what happened to you. You get to hate the sin perpetrated against you. God hates sin too. He loves the sinner, but he hates sin.

You may also experience other emotions, such as guilt, sadness, and grief. You have to feel the emotions and let yourself grieve if you want to get to the other side. Eventually, forgiveness will be required. We will talk more about that topic later, but for now, begin the process of forgiveness. It will not happen overnight.

Confront your offender. It may or may not be helpful to confront the person who hurt you. Before you go to the person face to face, you should ask yourself a few questions. Is the person emotionally stable and safe? Would you be emotionally and physically safe around them? Would the person use what you say to hurt you in the future? Are they emotionally able to hear what you need to say? Do they have health issues that would make confronting them a threat to their health or life? Are they still present and available? If confronting the person would cause more harm than good, refrain from a face to face situation.

The person you need to confront may not be available. In the case you cannot confront your offender face to face, the next best way is to confront the person in your own thoughts. This might be accomplished by writing them a letter you do not send, or your counselor may have you talk to them as if they were your offender.

Ask Jesus for help. Ask Jesus to walk with you through the pain and memories. Sometimes when we can't keep walking, he picks us up and carries us. He will calm the child's fear in you and hold you when you cry. With Christ, you don't have to walk through it alone.

"Then they cry out to the Lord in their trouble, and He brings them out of their distresses. He calms the storm, so that its waves are still." (Psalm 107:28-29 NKJV)

"For you have been a strength to the poor, strength to the needy in his distress, a refuge from the storm, a shade from the heat." (Isaiah 25:4 NKJV)

Here's where the healing starts, my friend. It starts with reframing the past. Don't let any more time pass by without beginning the process. Stop existing and start healing.

One of my biggest regrets in life is procrastinating doing the hard work it took to heal because I was too afraid. I wasted years struggling through life when I could have been thriving like I am now. Take the steps towards healing and into a restored life.

SESSION EIGHT REFLECTION QUESTIONS

Is emotional weight taking its toll on you physically? Explain.

Do you feel out of control or stuck in fear from past memories? Describe the memories and how they make you feel stuck in fear.

What does it mean to have hidden memories?

Do you feel like your childhood is foggy and unclear? Explain.

Do you have strange feelings about certain rooms or places in your past?

Do you strongly identify with people from a traumatic past? Do you understand why? Explain.

Do you need to begin asking relatives about your past? Who will you speak to and what will you ask them? Explain.

What do you need to take to God in prayer to understand your past?

Do you need to start by talking to a counselor? Who will you talk to?

Ask Jesus for the help you need in a prayer below

SESSION NINE

We Were Created to Be Dependent

Dependency. What have you heard about this word? You hear a lot about dependency in the media. It's the age of information. If you want to know anything about anything, just drop it in a computer search engine.

Common Terms:

>   issues with dependency
>   dependency problems
>   drug-dependent
>   dependent on alcohol
>   co-dependent

The list is long; these are just a few of the top, most identifiable terms. Actually, I searched the topic of dependency and here are a few terms you might not have thought of:

>   emotional dependence
>   psychological dependence
>   opioid dependence

Dependency is most always thought of as a bad thing. Dependency on drugs, alcohol, or other people. We have *issues* with dependency. It paints a bad impression of something unwanted. We think, "Who wants to be dependent? Not me!" I look at dependency on drugs and alcohol and know it's something that eventually leads to a bad outcome.

But is this the only way to think about dependency? Should we immediately react negatively to the idea of dependency? Is being dependent on something always bad? This is food for thought and something we will explore deeper this session.

According to Webster's dictionary, "dependent" is defined as influenced, controlled, or determined by something else; relying for support or aid; addicted.[1]

This says that when we are controlled by something or determined by something else, we are dependent. Also, if I *depend* on something or someone for support or aid, I am considered dependent.

To "depend" means to be influenced or determined by something else; to have trust; to rely on; to rely on for support or aid.[2]

When we consider the issue of dependency, we automatically think negatively. But the question is this: Can depending on something or someone be a good thing? Can we have a paradigm shift concerning dependency? Sometimes we get so focused in a direction, we don't see the forest for the trees. Let's open our minds to think in a new way about the subject.

Today, I want to show you a new, positive way to look at the idea of dependency. It's not bad to be influenced by something; just make sure it's the correct thing.

A New Way to Look at Dependency

To depend on or rely on someone for support is not a bad thing. Babies depend on their parents for food, shelter, and love. Parent's bathe, feed, and tend to all the needs of an infant. Until a child grows up enough to begin doing some things on its own, the parent supplies all a child needs. Babies are born trusting their parents; they have no other choice. Dependency for a baby is a very good thing. They get all their needs met as long as the one they are dependent upon is trustworthy.

Just like for a baby, dependency is something positive and necessary for us. But unlike a baby, we get to choose what we become dependent on.

We are born with the need to be dependent. It's built into us to crave dependency. First, we are dependent on our parents. Then as we shift from childhood into adulthood, we are to become dependent on God. Unfortunately, most of us do not get taught the message of shifting dependency from our parents onto God. Instead, we are taught to pull up our bootstraps and be independent. We learn to lean on ourselves and make our own decisions, which is not God's plan. Being independent is just another way of saying self-dependent, which can get us into trouble.

"Not that we are competent in anything for ourselves, but our competence comes from God." (2 Corinthians 3:5)

If we choose not to be dependent on God (like a small child), we instead become dependent on other things. In the Garden of Eden, man was created to be fully dependent on God. When the fall of mankind happened, it broke our connection to God and our dependency on him. Dependency on God is no longer automatic, but something we have to choose.

Our disconnection has left a void inside us only God is able to fill. We either choose to fill the void with God, or we will fill it with other things. Those other things may give us some amount of satisfaction and fill us temporarily, but only God can fill the void permanently.

You *will* be dependent on something or someone. It's just a matter of what you allow yourself to become dependent on. Will you turn your dependency toward God and fill the void permanently, or will you allow yourself to be controlled and consumed by the dependency on other things? That's the question you have to answer.

If you choose to depend on God, he will work with you to root out all other things controlling you. He will use his power to help you overcome. But without dependency on God, you are left to deal with your addictions and compulsion in your own power. And like we said in earlier weeks, we need supernatural power to change things, and that power doesn't come from us. Supernatural power comes from God.

Dependency on Things Other Than God

Dependency on other things will show up in drugs, alcohol, food, cigarettes, sex, a person in our life, our children, our parents, gambling, our pets, need for approval, drive for power, pornography, our job, computer usage, phone usage, television usage, social media usage, and so on. The list goes on and on. Did you ever see the television show *My Strange Addiction*? One of the previews showed a woman who was addicted to chalk. Just the preview was enough for me. But it shows that dependency can take on almost any form.

Drugs, alcohol, food, gambling, and sex are some of the biggest additions we hear about, but a person can become dependent on just about anything. If we allow ourselves to rely on something or someone other than God, we can essentially become dependent on it. Life is full of things for us to be dependent on as a substitute for depending on God.

Personally, I have used many things to avoid depending on God. Early in my life I depended on drugs and alcohol to provide a way of escape from the pain of a trauma-filled childhood. It wasn't until I turned to God for help when I was able to loosen pain's grip on me, stop escaping, and start healing my past. Early on in my Christian walk, I was dependent on cigarettes. After I kicked the smoking habit, I found I also had a dependency to Diet Coke. You may think it silly to consider my Diet Coke drinking as a dependency, but it really was. I couldn't go without it, which means I relied on it. Removing it from my life was difficult.

Now I find myself sometimes slipping back into the mode of using other things to help me deal with my feelings. When unwelcome feelings creep in, I want to find a substitute instead of depending on God. Those substitutes can be anything from food or shopping, to television and computer games. Sometimes I have to consciously remind myself not to use other things and go directly to God with my feelings. Dependency is a daily, hourly, minute-by-minute thing. Sometimes dependency on God comes easier than other times. It's a case-by-case issue. This time I will depend on God. Next time, again, I will depend on God instead of other things.

Some people take the position of belief that we don't really need God to have a fulfilling life. Maybe for a time. But it never lasts. We all run into things outside our power and ability to control. If we want true freedom from the addictions that plague our world, the only way to have it is by putting our dependency back where it belongs. We put our dependency on God and kick addiction out the door through his power, not our own. I'm not saying it will always be easy. In fact, it can be really hard to shift our dependency. But it's the only way to real, lasting freedom.

Dependency on things other than God spirals us downward, while dependency on God spirals us upward. You have to ask yourself, "Do I want my life to spiral up or down?" Downward-spiraling behaviors often look and feel enjoyable for a time, but eventually they end up controlling us. They eventually lead to an unsuccessful, out-of-balance life. At the bottom of the downward spiral our life is completely out of control and destructive. We can spiral up with God or down without him. The choice is ours.

How We Can Put Our Dependency on God

Let's walk through some Scriptures. They hold the keys within them to help us get the support and power needed to overcome obstacles in our life.

"Remain in me, as I also remain in you. No branch can bear fruit by itself; it must remain in the vine. Neither can you bear fruit unless you remain in me. I am the vine; you are the branches. If you remain in me and I in you, you will bear much fruit; apart from me you can do nothing." (John 15:4–5)

Jesus was in his final hours and still teaching his disciples. He knew what lay ahead for him the following day. He loved his disciples dearly. The night before his death, he spent the evening at the table with his twelve most loved for a last meal. Instead of worrying about what he would endure the following day, he was observing the traditional Passover meal. Jesus was concerned to the very end about his disciples and continued teaching until it was time for him to leave.

Remain in Jesus

Remain in me, and I in you, he tells them. *Remain in me…* what curious words for him to use. It means, *stand fast in me, stay in me, and reside in me.*

And I in you. He was telling them to stay residing in him and he would stand fast in them also.

Then he goes on to describe what he means with the word picture of a vine and its branches. In Israel during the New Testament time period, vineyards were commonplace. The example of a vine and its branches would have been something very familiar. Unlike us, they didn't go to the grocery store to get their produce. The process of tending to a vineyard would have been something most everyone would understand.

Jesus tells us, *"No branch can bear fruit by itself; it must remain in the vine. Neither can you bear fruit unless you remain in me."* If you take a branch and break it off the vine, it dies. The vine carries everything the branch needs to survive. A vine has water and nutrients; it supplies the branches with all it needs to thrive. It's not the branch which creates and produces fruit; it's the conductor used by the vine to produce fruit. What Jesus is saying is life for our spirit comes from our ability to remain in Christ. Daily remaining, recommitting, and resubmitting to his direction bears good things in our life.

"I am the vine; you are the branches. If you remain in me, and I in you, you will bear much fruit; apart from me you can do nothing." We can apply the example of fruit to many areas of our life, but for today's purpose, let's say the fruit is our ability to leave some addiction, habit, or hurt behind. Maybe it's our ability to live as God calls us to live free from our past behaviors and thinking.

If what Jesus is saying is true, we cannot accomplish freedom without him. He said, *if we remain in Him, we bear much fruit, but without him we can do nothing.* That's a strong statement. In this example, the fruit we bear by remaining in Jesus is freedom—the ability to leave behind our addiction, hurt, habit, past behavior, or wrong thinking.

Lean into God

"Come to me, all you who are weary and burdened, and I will give you rest. Take my yoke upon you and learn from me, for I am gentle and humble in heart, and you will find rest for your souls. For my yoke is easy and my burden is light." (Matthew 11:28–30)

While Jesus was teaching among the multitudes, he tells them to come to him for the rest they need when they are weary and feel burdened. We try and we labor to do and be, but instead of our burdens being lighter, they get heavier. Do your burdens feel heavy? Are you tired of trying so hard?

Have you ever thought, "Why does it have to be so hard?" I have. I've asked God that question so many times. Every time his answer is the same, *Lean into me, come to me. Take my yoke, not your own.*

Jesus tells us to come to him. He will give us the rest we need. *"Take my yoke,"* he says. *"Learn from me." "My yoke is easy." "My burden is light."*

A yoke is a wooden collar used in farming. You hook a team of two oxen or other animals together with a yoke so both will pull the plow behind them together in unison. The yoke is curved and fitted to the neck of the animal to prevent pain or discomfort while they carried the plow blade. Submission to the yoke allowed the burden of hauling to be equally distributed, lightening the load for the animals.

What Jesus is saying is when we are yoked to him, remaining in him, he will pull your weight. You get his part of the weight, which is easier, because he's already taken care of it all. You can rest because he has it under control. He is pulling the weight; his shoulders can handle the load.

Find Rest for Your Soul

Jesus wants rest for your soul. He says *learn from me, I am gentle and humble. I can give you the rest you so desperately need.*

Don't you need rest for your soul? Are you tired of pushing and struggling, trying to fix your life? Jesus says,

Remain in me.

Find rest for your soul.

Place your dependency in me.

Stop trying everything else and just depend on me.

One more lesson to go, my friend. You are doing great. I am proud of you! Lean on Jesus and let him carry you through the rest of the process. You were created to depend on him; let him do what comes natural for him.

SESSION NINE REFLECTION QUESTIONS

Explain what it means to be dependent.

How can dependency be a good thing?

Explain what it means for you personally to be dependent on God.

How can dependency on other things show up in a person's life?

How has dependency on other things shown up in your own life?

Explain what it means to spiral downward or spiral upward.

What does it mean to remain in God?

Explain how you personally are going to remain in God to accomplish your own goals. Make a plan.

Are there things in your life that you are tired of struggling with? What are they?

Do you need rest for your soul? Write a prayer asking God for the rest you need.

SESSION TEN

Knowing Your Identity and Value

Who are you? When you think of this question, do you think of your name? A name is not *who* you are. It's a label given to you by your parents.

If I ask you again, "Who are you?" do you answer with, "I'm a (occupation); *teacher, cashier, truck driver?*" Or did you think, "I work at (place of occupation)?" That's still not who you are; that's what you do or where you work.

If I ask you one more time, "Who are you?" do you answer, "I'm an American, I'm a resident of a city (fill in city), or I'm a Missouri resident?" Or did you answer with "I'm a Christian, I'm a Baptist, or I'm a Protestant?" This is still not who you are; it's where you live or your religious preference.

You are not your height or weight. You are not the color of your hair or the color of your eyes. These are descriptions of your appearance. If your hair color changes, if you gain or lose weight, it doesn't change who you are. It doesn't change your value or significance. Although we shouldn't identify ourselves by our appearance, we often do. We place our value on what job we hold or where we went to school. We consider ourselves more important by the amount of beauty or success we have.

Placing our identity on external things is dangerous because they don't really answer the question of who we are. External circumstances can change, meaning our identity can change. When we lose our beauty, we think our value decreases, and somehow we are less significant. When we lose that high-paying job, we believe we are less successful and therefore less worthy of value.

Let's start there, valuing ourselves because of whom we belong to, not who everyone else would want or expect us to be. We are significant because God says we are. So when you are asked "Who are you?" respond with this:

"My name is (insert your name), a uniquely created child of the King of all creation."

Have you allowed who you are be determined by what you do? Maybe it's time to turn the tables, letting what you do be determined by who you are.

You Are a New Creation

"He came to that which was his own, but his own did not receive him. Yet to all who received him, to those who believed in his name, he gave the right to become children of God." (John 1:11–12)

"For you have been born again, not of perishable seed, but of imperishable, through the living and enduring Word of God." (1 Peter 1:23)

When we accept Jesus Christ as our savior, we are born again. Our Spirit is made new and we become children of God. We are no longer identified by our past. God no longer sees our sin and identifies who we are by the mistakes we have made. We have been made new and he sees us as clean, pure, and white as snow. This is our new life and who we are. We have to learn to live out of our new identity and value ourselves by what God says about us. Our significance comes by who he says we are.

Colossians 3:9–10 tells us we *have put on the new self, which is being renewed in knowledge in the image of its Creator.* Since we have taken off the old self, we have a new one on now. Our new self is alive spiritually and our soul is now being renewed by learning the way we were created to be. By studying the word of God, we gain wisdom, understanding, and knowledge. It then renews our mind, will, and emotions so they align to the image and character of God.

All humanity suffers from a need for significance which is only available to us through God. We must learn to get our sufficiency and value from the Creator, not other things. We are the greatest of all the creations he created. Our value doesn't come from our beauty, giftedness, talent, or intelligence. True personal value comes from knowing you are a child of God and the growth of your character in Christ. A masterpiece has no value unless the painter who created it is a world-class artist. God created you as his masterpiece, and your tremendous value comes because of his ability he placed within you.

You cannot know the mind of Christ unless you have given your life to him. With the acceptance of Jesus Christ comes the implanted Holy Spirit who gives us the understanding to become transformed into Christ's image. It is through a growing relationship that we increase in character and are changed inside and out.

Who Are You in Christ?

The truth about who you are in Christ makes all the difference in your success with handling the challenges and struggles in life. It is imperative to your growth and maturity that you believe God's truth about who you are. In the book *Victory Over the Darkness*, Neil T. Anderson lists what Scripture says about your identity. Take a look at the exhaustive list below.

I Am Accepted

John 1:12	I am Christ's friend.
Romans 5:1	I have been justified.
1 Corinthians 6:17	I am united with the Lord, and I am one spirit with him.
1 Corinthians 6:20	I have been bought with a price. I belong to God.
1 Corinthians 12:27	I am a member of Christ's body.
Ephesians 1:1	I am a saint.
Ephesians 1:5	I have been adopted as God's child.
Ephesians 2:18	I have direct access to God through the Holy Spirit.
Colossians 1:14	I have been redeemed and forgiven of all my sins.
Colossians 2:10	I am complete in Christ.

I Am Secure

Romans 8:1–2	I am free from condemnation.
Romans 8:28	I am assured that all things work together for good.
Romans 8:31–34	I am free from any condemning charges against me.
Romans 8:38–39	I cannot be separated from the love of God.
2 Corinthians 1:21–22	I have been established, anointed, and sealed by God.
Philippians 1:6	I am confident that the good work God has begun in me will be perfected.
Philippians 3:20	I am a citizen of heaven.
Colossians 3:3	I am hidden with Christ in God.
2 Timothy 1:7	I have not been given a spirit of fear but of power, love, and a sound mind.
Hebrews 4:16	I can find grace and mercy in time of need.
1 John 5:18	I am born of God, and the evil one cannot touch me.

I Am Significant

Matthew 5:13–14	I am the salt and light of the earth.
John 15:1, 5	I am a branch of the true vine, a channel of his life.
John 15:16	I have been chosen and appointed to bear fruit.
Acts 1:8	I am a personal witness of Christ.
1 Corinthians 3:16	I am God's temple.
2 Corinthians 5:17–21	I am a minister of reconciliation for God.
2 Corinthians 6:1	I am God's co-worker. (See also 1 Corinthians 3:9)
Ephesians 2:6	I am seated with Christ in the heavenly realm.

Ephesians 2:10	I am God's workmanship.
Ephesians 3:12	I may approach God with freedom and confidence.
Philippians 4:13	I can do all things through Christ who strengthens me.

Do you have trouble believing you have great worth?

Are some of these scriptures difficult to claim as your own?

Go back through the list, and ask yourself, "Do I claim this as a description of me?" "Do I believe this is true about me?"

If there are some descriptions you are unable accept or believe, you have lies blocking the truth from being implanted in you. Now is the time to figure out what lies you believe and replace them with the truth, because you can't live beyond what you believe. Now is the time to change what you believe so you can live in freedom and truth about yourself.

Blessings You Have in Christ

Because we are in Christ, we have access to a tremendous amount of blessing in our lives. Read the following list slowly and take it in as truth. These blessings God has given you are all yours to claim. God says these things about you since you are his in Christ.

By the grace of God...	**Supporting Scripture**
I have been justified, completely forgiven, and made righteous.	Romans 5:1
I died with Christ and died to the power of sin's rule over my life.	Romans 6:1–6
I am free forever from condemnation.	Romans 8:1
I have been placed into Christ by God's doing.	1 Corinthians 1:30
I have received the Spirit of God into my life that I might know the things freely given to me by God.	1 Corinthians 2:12
I have been given the mind of Christ.	1 Corinthians 2:16
I have been bought with a price; I am not my own; I belong to God.	1 Corinthians 6:19, 20

I have been established, anointed, and sealed by God in Christ, and I have been given the Holy Spirit as a pledge guaranteeing our inheritance to come.	2 Corinthians 1:21, 22; Ephesians 1:13, 14
Since I have died, I no longer live for myself, but for Christ.	2 Corinthians 5:14, 15
I have been made righteous.	2 Corinthians 5:21
I have been crucified with Christ, and it is no longer I who live, but Christ lives in me. The life I am now living is Christ's life.	Galatians 2:20
I have been blessed with every spiritual blessing.	Ephesians 1:3
I was chosen in Christ before the foundation of the world to be holy, and I am without blame before him.	Ephesians 1:4
I was predestined (determined by God) to be adopted as God's son or daughter.	Ephesians 1:5
I have been redeemed and forgiven, and I am a recipient of his lavish grace.	Ephesians 1:7, 8
I have been made alive together with Christ.	Ephesians 2:5
I have been raised up and seated with Christ in heaven.	Ephesians 2:6
I have direct access to God through the Spirit.	Ephesians 2:18
I may approach God with boldness, freedom, and confidence.	Ephesians 3:12
I have been rescued from the domain of Satan's rule and transferred to the kingdom of Christ.	Colossians 1:13
I have been redeemed and forgiven of all my sins. The debt against me has been cancelled.	Colossians 1:14, 2:14
Christ himself is in me.	Colossians 1:27
I am firmly rooted in Christ and am now being built in him.	Colossians 2:7
I have been made complete in Christ.	Colossians 2:10
I have been spiritually circumcised.	Colossians 2:11
I have been buried, raised, and made alive with Christ.	Colossians 2:12, 13

I died with Christ and I have been raised up with Christ. My life is now hidden in Christ with God. Christ is now my life.	Colossians 3:1–4
I have been given a spirit of power, love, and self-discipline.	2 Timothy 1:7
I have been saved and set apart according to God's doing.	2 Timothy 1:9; Titus 3:5
Because I am sanctified and one with the Sanctifier, he is not ashamed to call me brother.	Hebrews 2:11
I have the right to come boldly before the throne of God to find mercy and grace in time of need.	Hebrews 4:16
I have been given exceedingly great and precious promises by God of which I am a partaker of God's divine nature.	2 Peter 1:4

God's Restoring Plan for You

God has a plan, and it's all about restoring you. Claim every bit of it so you can live as who he created you to be.

Along with all the promises above, there are so many more in Scripture. One I cling to is Jeremiah 29:11, which says he has a plan for us. Not just any plan but one to prosper, not harm us, to give us hope and a future. He has a plan for you if you follow him, and it's full of hope.

In Joel 2:25–27, God promises the Israelites he will restore all the crops eaten by the locust to work wonders for his people, and never again will they be shamed. What this means for us as part of God's people is that we get to receive the same promise as the Israelites did. God will restore what destruction tried to steal, and he will remove every ounce of shame along with it. Stay in pursuit of restoration and receive every promise he has made.

Well done, dear one! You have reached the end of this course. But it's just the beginning of healing and a life well lived. I have full confidence that with the help of God you can find more than just a scrap of goodness in the future.

You can have full restoration.

You can have healing.

Be blessed as you live as a child of God.

SESSION TEN REFLECTION QUESTIONS

Do you identify yourself by the way you look or what you do? Explain.

Are you ready to begin allowing God to determine who you are? How will you start doing that?

Pick your two favorite scriptures under *I Am Accepted* and write them below

Pick your two favorite scriptures under *I Am Secure* and write them below.

Pick your two favorite scriptures under *I Am Significant* and write them below.

Do you have trouble believing you have great worth to God? Explain Why.

Pick two scriptures from *By the Grace of God* which mean something to you and write them below.

Why do these two scriptures mean something to you?

Use the space below to write a prayer asking God to help you know who you are.

ENDNOTES

SESSION 3
[1] Kandy Jackson, Lee's Summit, Missouri, Counselor at Epic Counseling Group

SESSION 5
[1] *Webster's New World College Dictionary – Third Edition Completely Updated*
Copyright © 1997, 1996, 1994, 1991, 1988 by Simon & Schuster, Inc.
[2] Strong, James, 1822-1894
The Strongest Strong's exhaustive concordance of the Bible / James Strong -21st century ed., fully rev. and corrected / by John R. Kohlenberger III and James A. Swanson
[3] Strong, James, 1822-1894
The Strongest Strong's exhaustive concordance of the Bible / James Strong -21st century ed., fully rev. and corrected / by John R. Kohlenberger III and James A. Swanson
[4] *Webster's New World College Dictionary – Third Edition Completely Updated*
Copyright © 1997, 1996, 1994, 1991, 1988 by Simon & Schuster, Inc.

Session 6
[1] Seamands, David, *Healing for Damaged Emotions,* First published 1981, Scripture Press Publishers
[2] Karpman, Stephen, *The Life Drama Triangle,* Article first published in 1968 *as Karpman's Triangle*
[3] *Webster's New World College Dictionary – Third Edition Completely Updated*
Copyright © 1997, 1996, 1994, 1991, 1988 by Simon & Schuster, Inc.
[4] Graham, Linda, MFT. Resources for Recovering Resilience
www.lindagraham-mft.net /triangle-victim-rescuer-persecutor-get/

Session 9
[1] *Webster's New World College Dictionary – Third Edition Completely Updated*
Copyright © 1997, 1996, 1994, 1991, 1988 by Simon & Schuster, Inc.
[2] *Webster's New World College Dictionary – Third Edition Completely Updated*
Copyright © 1997, 1996, 1994, 1991, 1988 by Simon & Schuster, Inc.